Babies
Can Talk

Books by Dr. Marilyn Daniels

Dancing with Words: Signing for Hearing Children's Literacy
Benedictine Roots in the Development of Deaf Education: Listening with the Heart
The Dance in Christianity: A History of Religious Dance Through the Ages
Toddlers At Play

DVDs by We Sign

Babies and Toddlers 2
Baby Songs
Play Time
Fun Time
ABCs
Numbers
Colors
Animals
Rhymes
More Animals
Classroom Favorites
Santa's Favorite Christmas Songs
Christmas Carols
Patriotic Songs

Sign
to
Speak

Babies
Can Talk

[signature]

Marilyn Daniels, PhD
Georgia Frawley, MA
Ken Frawley

For Mimi Houston:
My very best wishes
on your independent
project on sign
language.
Sincerely,
D. Daniels
August 2010

For my great-grandsons
Elijah John and Anthony Laurence
and all young children

Marilyn Daniels

Production Associates, Inc.
1206 W. Collins Ave.
Orange, CA 92867
www.wesign.com

Printed in the United States of America

Publisher's Cataloging-in-Publication data

Daniels, Marilyn.
    Babies can talk : a practical guide for early communication through signing and fun activities / Marilyn Daniels, PhD, Georgia Frawley, MA, Ken Frawley.
    p. cm.
    Series: Sign to Speak
    Includes bibliographical references and index.
    ISBN 9781887120906
1. Sign language. 2. Nonverbal communication in children. 3. Infants–Language. 4. American Sign Language.
5. Sign language acquisition–Parent participation. I. Frawley, Georgia. II. Frawley, Ken. III. Title.

HV2474 .D25 2010
419/.1 22--dc22   2010920654

Executive Project Director: Mike Cash
Cover and interior design: Bryan Spencer
Photo Editing: Ben Marker
Copyediting: PeopleSpeak
Signing Models: Sarah Hogan and Jason Roehm
Photography: Bill Dean and Guy Cali
Original songs written by Ken Frawley: *How Many Legs, The Tiny Little Mouse, Where Is Baby, I See a Bunny, Five Little Fingers, Sleep Little Baby, Do You Hear the Ducky Sing, The Pretty Little Pony*

Contents

Part 2   How to Sign with Your Baby

Part 3   Signing in Your Everyday Life and Activities

Preface

Sign language is now an internationally accepted way to communicate with hearing babies long before they can speak and to enhance their language growth. We believe that when parents are signing with babies (birth to 18 months), they need to focus on their children's abilities and use age-appropriate signs with them. *Sign to Speak: Babies Can Talk* was written specifically to teach parents how to use signing with their babies.

Imagine how wonderful it would be to know what your baby wants or what your baby needs or what your baby is thinking. Signing offers babies a unique opportunity to communicate with their hands before they develop the ability to speak. How great it would be to not feel frustrated time and time again with the "crying or tantrum guessing game." Consider the benefits of knowing what your baby wants. Signing offers you these benefits.

Best of all, signing works because it is an organic and natural part of human interaction, not just a passing fad. As babies develop they begin to use their hands to express themselves, even if signing is not taught to them. They reach for and grasp things, they push things away, and they even rub their ears when they have earaches. Babies naturally develop signs that parents understand, and by teaching them sign language parents are providing babies with a structured way to communicate. Signing allows babies to express their wants and needs while offering them an organic approach for communication, understanding, and language even before they can speak.

With more than 60 years of combined signing experience, we are providing parents and caregivers a proven, practical, fun, and informative approach to the use of American Sign Language, commonly known as ASL, with babies. Our "hands-on" concepts, easy-to-follow tips, and simple-to-learn signs require no previous signing knowledge or experience. All you need is the desire to engage in this playful and very beneficial activity with your baby.

There are so many compelling reasons for parents to sign with their babies, and it is our belief that involved parents are also informed parents. Therefore, within our book we also provide parents with research, science, theories, and historical perspectives about the use of ASL. The information provided here is intended to empower babies through signing and to engender in parents and caregivers a steadfast support for using signs not only when their children are babies but also as their children grow.

Acknowledgments

Since my initial research, examining the value of ASL for hearing children, I've received assistance and encouragement from the Deaf community. During the intervening years, as my research expanded to include hearing people from infancy to old age, this Deaf co-culture has consistently been open to sharing their non-verbal manual language with me. Their support began in the early nineties in Pennsylvania at the Scranton State School for the Deaf. It was there that Deaf mothers of hearing children allowed their off-spring to participate in my very first research study in this area. This support continued and took on national and international ramifications when I was invited to participate in state, regional and national conferences of the Deaf in California, New York, New Jersey, Pennsylvania, Michigan, Maryland, South Carolina, and Utah. During the summer of 2003, I was invited to teach at Nagoya University in Nagoya, Japan. How thrilling to find the local Deaf community supportive and attending my lectures in this foreign country. The Japanese were intent in learning how educators in the United States used ASL to enhance communication and English language development in hearing populations. My work with the American Deaf community culminated in an invitation to share my research in Calgary, Canada. At this national conference of Deaf educators the participants, both deaf and hearing, were excited to learn about the ASL techniques I wrote about and adapt them with their children and students. The Deaf community in the United States and throughout the world has remained supportive of my work for nearly twenty years. I acknowledge with gratitude their generosity and willingness to share their language, American Sign Language, with me and the rest of the hearing world.

Marilyn Daniels, PhD

There are many people that have contributed their time and effort to this Sign to Speak project. Mike Cash, president of Production Associates, Inc., helped direct and produce this book. Ben Marker created the artwork for the signs. Sharon Goldinger edited the manuscript and guided us through all aspects of the project. Bryan Spencer designed the cover and layout. Sarah Hogan and Jason Roehm were our signing models, and Bill Dean and Guy Cali provided photography. Finally, it has been a great pleasure working with Marilyn Daniels, a true professional and kindred spirit.

Ken and Georgia Frawley

Introduction

Babies can easily communicate with their parents and caregivers—if they have a language to use. By using sign language, you and your baby will be able to communicate long before the baby is ready to talk. This book will show you how. And you'll discover the many other benefits of signing: accelerated language growth, increased IQ scores, enhanced memory and recall, and more. Best of all, you'll be building a stronger bond between you and your baby as you have fun signing together.

Sign to Speak: Babies Can Talk has been written to help parents foster early language and vocabulary growth with babies and to reduce parent-child communication frustrations through the use of sign language, specifically American Sign Language, commonly known as ASL. It is designed such that you can use as few or as many signs as you wish when signing with your baby. We believe that for inexperienced signers, what's important is not the quantity of signs you use but the quality of the words you choose to sign and how you use them with your baby.

All of the signs, tips, and other information in this book have been used successfully with babies. Best of all, you do not have to know a thing about signing to reap its rich rewards. Just follow our instructions, introduce just a few signs at a time, and create some fun signing activities to reinforce the learning and you'll be on your way to providing early learning and communication to your baby. We have separated signing with babies from signing with toddlers because there is a vast difference between the needs and use of language for a baby and the expanding, if not exploding, world of language for a toddler. We know you will find signing with your baby to be a rewarding experience, one that you will want to continue as your child becomes a toddler, preschooler, and older child.

You will discover that using sign language with a baby actually helps the child acquire an advanced understanding of language itself. When babies begin to understand the signs, they will soon be aware that there are two ways to signify an action or object. For instance, MORE can be spoken and they can hear it, or MORE can be signed and they can see it. A baby who recognizes this is becoming what linguists call metalinguistic. In addition, signing babies have a clearer perception of the world around them. This early understanding of the environment seems to create an enthusiasm for learning.

Using ASL eliminates many of the barriers in the communication channel between parents and children. Signing reduces crying and screaming and eases frustrations as it fosters more readily understood exchanges. Signing with a baby becomes fun for both baby and caregiver and establishes lifelong bonds between them.

How This Book Came About

Dr. Marilyn Daniels's interest grew out of her interactions with some of her graduate students in a communication theories course. Many of the students made extra money serving as sign language interpreters for hearing children of Deaf parents. They would often attend parent-teacher conferences at elementary schools and interpret the teachers' comments for the Deaf parents. The graduate students were surprised to learn that these schoolchildren were doing extremely well in all of their language arts classes. "Why would this be the case?" they asked. These children came from homes where little or no English was spoken, and they had all learned ASL as their first language. The graduate students said, "It doesn't make sense."

Marilyn tended to agree with them and had no good explanation for this. But her interest was piqued, and she began to delve more deeply into the puzzle. Corroborating interviews with interpreters in Pennsylvania, New Jersey, and Connecticut who worked with hearing children of Deaf parents indicated that this was not an isolated phenomenon. Armed with that knowledge, she decided to do her own research.

Her first study, "ASL as a Factor in Acquiring English," was published in *Sign Language Studies* in 1993. This research examined the size of the vocabularies of 14 hearing children in Pennsylvania ranging in age from 2 years, 10 months to 13 years, 6 months. The children all had normal hearing. They learned ASL as babies and were fluent in both ASL and English. With the exception of one child, who was the daughter of an interpreter, they all had one or more Deaf parents.

Their vocabularies were measured with the Peabody Vocabulary Test. This is a well-respected test of receptive English vocabulary that has been used by educators in its successive editions for more than 50 years. Because this test's outcomes are age referenced, it can be administered to anyone between the ages of 2 years, 6 months and 40. The expected score for someone with an average vocabulary is 100. The mean derived score of the 14 children was 109.57, significantly higher than scores expected from a randomly selected sample. This result clearly demonstrated that children who learned ASL as babies acquired a far larger English vocabulary than would be expected of typical children.

These results were very exciting because they indicated that knowing ASL offered strong language and literacy benefits to hearing youngsters. The "wow" factor of these numbers catapulted Marilyn into doing further research. She began a quest to discover whether similar results would occur in different populations with other babies and young children.

Now, years later and after countless hours of research, the results of her efforts have demonstrated that ASL offers a myriad of educational advantages to children ranging from infancy through age 13. All of Marilyn's interactions with parents, grandparents, teachers, and the beneficiaries of this ongoing effort, the babies and children who have learned ASL, have led her to the view that ASL is an almost magical approach for language learning. Her book *Dancing with Words: Signing for Hearing Children's Literacy* has become one of the most widely used and quoted resources for signing with children of all ages.

Memory and recall, early communication, language development, and frustration reduction through the use of American Sign Language were concepts Georgia Frawley had been aware of for years. She first encountered the use of ASL with children when she worked as a dorm counselor at the California School for the Deaf in Riverside. This was an amazing experience for her: in one day she easily went from knowing no signs to knowing more than 30.

Years later, she used the signs she had learned at the School for the Deaf, in combination with speaking, as her way to communicate with her own infants. She believed that signing was a simple way to reinforce language development. However, when her children began signing words when they were as young as 8 months old, she realized that signing provided them with a language skill. This allowed her children to tell her what they wanted without crying or screaming.

Georgia has been teaching high school classes in the area of child development for over 30 years. During her career, she taught students in a Careers with Children class, where she prepared them for working with young children. Included in the curriculum were theories by renowned psychologists Erik Erikson, Abraham Maslow, and Howard Gardner. They all agree that when working with children, a caregiver needs to focus on the children's developmental stages, meet their needs, include as many learning opportunities as possible, and encourage children to maximize their learning potential. Georgia has found that signing, especially when incorporated with music, is a surefire way to engage children and enable all children to be successful.

Georgia also developed and supervised an on-campus day-care center at her high school and worked closely with various day-care centers and preschools in her area. Her day-care parents and Child Development students cared for children ranging in age from 6 weeks to 4 years old. Signing with these children became part of the routine. Over the years she has learned many positive stories and comments about the use of signing with young children.

Ken Frawley graduated from college with the intention of becoming an elementary school teacher in California. He began to perform music and storytelling programs for children in preschools, in elementary schools, at libraries, and at various other community events. After one of his concerts, a signing friend said, "It would be nice if Deaf and hearing children had something they could do together." Ken decided to add singing and signing to his concerts.

To his amazement, he found that children, even a year later, remembered many of the signs he had showed them. After a little bit of research, it became very clear to Ken that we all learn and remember better when we are involved in what we are being taught. We have known for thousands of years that learning involving a variety of our senses is a powerful memory and recall tool. Sign language and songs engage children visually and verbally, through movement, music, and more.

In the early 1990s Ken cofounded Production Associates, Inc., and began producing ASL products for children of all ages. The products he helped produce were designed to provide members of each age group with a fun way to include ASL in their lives while learning and remembering a lot of vocabulary and educational concepts. All the titles he helped to create were designed to be interactive and to provide clear instruction for parents, teachers, and caregivers so that they could engage in this activity with their children and keep the visual images fun and interesting.

Ken helped design the original Say, Sing and Sign video series, which featured ASL because of Georgia's foundation in that language. Ken and Georgia were two of the pioneers in the field of signing for hearing children. They began by providing preschool and elementary school children with videos of songs and signs for learning the basics: *ABC, Numbers, Colors, Rhymes,* and *Animals.* Ultimately they changed the series name to We Sign and added the *Babies & Toddlers* video so parents could learn to use signs for early communication and learning.

For years, Ken and Georgia have worked hard to educate the country on the benefits of signing for hearing children. They have lectured and taught parents, educators, and caregivers across the United States the We Sign concepts about signing with children. As part of the We Sign team, they have coauthored this book in an effort to continue empowering parents, teachers, caregivers, and children not only with the foundation for developing language skills and a way to ease communication frustrations but also with a playful way to support early learning and language growth.

The authors have received positive reactions and accolades from parents, teachers, and caregivers about the use of signing with all children. They firmly believe that if you give this manual language a try with your baby and continue to use it as your child grows, you will become as enthusiastic as we are. You will also see your child experience all of the educational advantages outlined in this book. Plus, you will come to know that sign language offers an intangible enhancement to the communication and language development process.

How to Use This Book

This book is broken into three parts and an appendix. Part 1 provides research and information on why signing is a wonderful activity for all children, the science of why signing with babies works, and a general explanation on why we suggest using ASL. Much of this part is based on the work of Dr. Marilyn Daniels, one of America's leading experts and researchers on signing with hearing children.

Part 2 provides the three "Jump Start on Smart" signs along with tips for signing with your baby. Through years of working with parents and caregivers, these three signs have proven to be the most effective as they go directly to the wants and needs of babies. This part also offers you over 30 additional words to use with your baby. We have included helpful tips and detailed strategies for successful signing. You can follow our strategies or choose your own. Either way, you and your baby will reap the benefits of this wonderful activity.

Part 3 offers fun and practical signing activities, specially designed for use with babies. Each activity supports early communication and language development and offers a variety of ways to incorporate signing into your daily life. You will find songs and rhymes that you can chant, sing, or speak. You can also go to our Web site and download the music for you and your baby to enjoy.

The appendix features the Babies Can Talk Toolbox, which includes our quick-reference alphabetical glossary of all the signs in this book. You will also find useful pages of tips and other information that you can photocopy for your personal use, and give out or post to help everyone involved with your baby sign with you.

PART I

Why Sign with Your Baby?

Chapter 1
Communicating without Words

For babies, crying has always been part of the communication process. It has provided countless generations of parents with an indication that something is wrong. But parents didn't know exactly what was wrong until their babies could talk. Today, parents can incorporate sign language into their babies' lives. This nonverbal, physical language provides babies with the ability to communicate their wants, needs, and interests at a very early age, many months before they can talk. Imagine how wonderful it would be for babies to tell you, with signs, what is wrong, what they want, or even what they are interested in, giving you the opportunity to deal with it directly instead of guessing. In this chapter, you'll discover how signing can offer you and your child the ability to communicate without the screaming or crying tantrums and learn more about the many benefits that signing with babies can provide.

Why Babies Cry

For years, Georgia Frawley has been posing this question to the students in her Child Development classes: "Why do babies cry?" She has asked this question of thousands of students and always gets the same answers, which she then lists on the board: babies cry because they are hungry, sleepy, sick, lonely, hot, in pain, scared; they have a wet or messy diaper; they are uncomfortable; and so on.

When the students feel satisfied with their list, she asks the question again: "But why do babies cry?" After a prolonged silence, a student will finally offer this answer: "Because they can't talk!"

Yes! Babies cry because they have no other way to tell you that they need something. They have to get your attention and hope that you can figure out what's wrong. Most parents eventually do figure it out through trial and error. The baby's needs get met, and everyone is happy—until the next cry.

Spoken language is one of the hardest things for a person to learn. It takes a tremendous amount of fine muscle control (controlling the mouth, tongue, and lips). Infants have more control over the large muscles for gross motor movement before they gain fine motor movement. For example, babies can swipe their arms at a dangling mobile toy (gross motor movement) long before they can use their fingers to pick up a block (fine motor movement).

Crying and screaming does not have to be the way a baby communicates. Parents who teach their babies sign language provide them with a language skill that engages their physical abilities to express themselves. Babies can sign words and tell you what they want and need and greatly reduce crying and screaming frustrations.

The Benefits of Signing with Babies

Ever since American Sign Language has been used in the United States, many people have reported the benefits that hearing children received by learning ASL. Since the 1970s, researchers have been studying the effects of signing with babies, toddlers, preschoolers, and older children. These studies have demonstrated that hearing babies receive a wide variety of benefits.

- **Signing fosters early language growth.** Studies have demonstrated that children who sign can have twice the usable vocabulary when signed and spoken words are combined. Having this collection of words allows babies to discover more of their world because they can direct their parents' and caregivers' attention to the things they are interested in, want, or need.
- **Signing reduces parent-child communication frustrations.** Babies can sign words to their parents many months before they can speak. Instead of making you play the "crying guessing game" and having screaming temper tantrums, babies can let you know if they are hungry, if they want more, if they are all done, and much more as they grow.
- **Signing stimulates brain development.** The ability to use language aids in a baby's brain development. Signing stimulates the growth and connection of neurons and synapses, helping babies to acquire and remember more language.
- **Signing provides an interactive bonding activity.** Signing is an activity in which parents and babies are paying attention to each other. Signing is a visual language, so they must look at each other. The minutes here and there that parents spend signing turn into hours of meaningful and playful interaction. This interaction supports parent-child bonding that will grow and extend throughout their lifetimes.
- **Signing offers babies a language skill.** Babies can speak with signs before they can talk. Generally, babies begin to speak words when they're around 14 to 16 months old. Signing babies have been known to sign words as early as 6 months old. By the time signing babies begin to talk, they may already have a vocabulary of six, eight, or more words that they have been communicating for 3 to 6 months. Even after talking begins, the spoken words are often different than the signed words.
- **Signing enhances eye gaze.** Babies learn so much with their eyes as they watch their parents, look at objects in front of them, and view their world. Signing encourages babies to focus on specific objects and signs. Because of the visual nature of ASL, babies use their eyes to learn.
- **Signing develops fine and gross motor skills.** Because signing involves the use of fingers, hands, and arms, it helps babies develop control over the associated muscle groups as well as eye-hand coordination.
- **Signing strengthens memory retention and recall.** Signing helps babies learn words using a variety of learning styles. Because the words are stored in multiple parts of the brain, memory and recall are strengthened.

- **Signing builds confidence and positive self-esteem.** As babies become successful signers and communicators, they become more confident in themselves and their abilities. This confidence will continue to encourage an enthusiasm for learning and give them the knowledge that they can succeed.
- **Signing generates a real enthusiasm for learning.** Signing is fun and playful. When babies learn signs, they not only accomplish communication but also gain praise and support from those around them. This positive reinforcement for learning encourages them to learn more and more.

Why Use Signs with Your Baby?

The two inherent differences between learning a spoken language and learning a signed language both favor the signed language. The first difference is the external control. In a signed language, parents can easily mold and guide their baby's hands into the correct formation and movement of a sign. Comparable manipulation of a baby's speech mechanism is impossible. Second, and this is an important and significant difference, the parent and baby must be looking at each other to be able to understand the signs and communicate. For this reason, the quality of the communication is elevated.

Signing Has No Downside

Every sign your infant learns will help form new synapses. Your baby will not only know what an English word means and sounds like but also know what it feels like. The child will actually have a tactile memory of the word, will know what a word looks like, and will have a visual memory of it. From the first shared meaning, you and your baby will begin the socialization process. Your child will gain a larger vocabulary from signing and a clear understanding of each word. Your signing child will generally talk sooner than nonsigning babies and acquire a much larger usable vocabulary. Signing will encourage speech rather than delay it.

We do not believe that signing has any downside. Nor is there a correct way or an incorrect way to incorporate signing into your life. In this book we offer signs that we know foster early communication and have worked with parents for years. However, whatever you feel is best will undoubtedly work best for you and your baby.

Signing Success Story

Jennifer's daughter, Allison, began to tell her mother that she wanted to eat by signing EAT. She began signing at around 8 months old and would use the EAT sign anytime she was hungry. She would also sign EAT during meal times when she wanted more food. Jennifer began to feel strongly that signing was an ideal way for her baby to express herself.

By the time Allison was 12 months old, she was signing words like ALL DONE, SLEEP, and MORE. These were signs that Allison used to tell her mother what she wanted. Jennifer and her husband, Jeff, loved the fact that their baby was communicating with them in a way that allowed them to understand clearly. Allison knew what she wanted and could say it with signs.

Allison soon began to sign other fun words that Jennifer had been using with books and objects around the house. Allison could sign FISH, for the family goldfish, and she loved to sign BALL and BOOK when she saw her toy ball or a book. Jennifer and her husband knew that Allison had connected the signed words with the objects. The result was a very clear way for Allison to communicate what she was thinking or what she was interested in to her mom and dad.

As Allison grew, her signing vocabulary grew too. Later, when she began to talk, she continued to use signs as well. Often Allison could sign a word but not say it yet, and Jennifer reported that many of the other mothers were impressed with the range of Allison's vocabulary.

> *Jennifer and her husband came to understand that signing greatly enhanced their daughter's spoken vocabulary. But for them, one of the best benefits of signing was the frustration reduction that came from their understanding of what Allison wanted, needed, and was interested in.*

Organic Nature of Signing

The information we offer to you in this book, the signs we present to you, and the benefits we describe are not just the current fad for early learning. They are instead an integral part of human development. Using signs is an organic and natural way for babies to learn to use language. As they continue to communicate in this manner, they will develop spoken language earlier, and when they grow older, the signs they know will enhance their ability to read and write.

The use of sign is a clear and natural part of our human experience. Over the last one hundred years many scholars have believed that the use of sign predated speech and helped humanity develop into spoken and written languages. Think about how many signs are used to communicate every day. These signs are all around us. For example, we wave goodbye, point to objects, motion to come here, and shrug to say "I don't know." Traffic officers use signing to direct us to stop, go, and turn. During sporting events we see signs for a strike, for a player who was offside, or if there's been a personal foul or a change in the direction of play and much more. Signing for communication is part of our organic human nature.

Children do not develop the extensive use of spoken words until they approach two years of age or older. Prior to that age they can understand words and concepts. Children need to express themselves, but unless they are given a natural way to communicate, they are reduced to grabbing, pushing, crying, and whining. *Sign to Speak* provides babies with a natural and timeless way to use and grow their language skills. Signing feels comfortable and is a way of communicating that babies are physically able to do. Because this approach to communication is organic, many parents, teachers, and caregivers have found signing to be beneficial for children, their families, and their communities.

Conclusion

As you continue reading, it will become evident that introducing sign language to a baby at a young age makes a good deal of common sense. Babies are hungry for communication and have the ability to understand and use words. Infants want to interact with the people with whom they come into contact. Babies, until recently, have had no way to communicate except for crying. Sign language's great gift to babies and their parents is a manual communication skill. This interactive skill and behavior will provide early learning, social, and linguistic benefits for your baby.

Chapter 2
How Babies Learn

Humanity has known for thousands of years that the more involved someone is in the learning process, the better the information learned is retained and the more available it is for future use. Signing is a rich learning activity for children. If you study the works of modern theorists such as Howard Gardner, Erik Erikson, and Abraham Maslow, you will come to the same conclusion as millions of other parents: developmentally, signing with a baby makes sense.

A Baby's Brain

Let's begin by looking at your baby. What do you notice? Perhaps first you see that your baby's head is pretty big in comparison to the size of the body. The neck is undoubtedly short, as are the arms and legs, with little curled-up hands and feet. The baby appears to be aware of hands, which are almost always moving. The face is often animated with eyes wide open, already starting to meet your gaze. The baby's mouth moves and will turn toward the breast or bottle if offered. The infant reacts to sounds and will sometimes jump if startled when resting or sleeping. The baby also cries at times, often very loudly.

What do we understand about babies? Our ideas about their abilities are constantly evolving. For instance, today we know that babies are more aware of the world than most psychologists once thought.

Brain Cells and Synapses

A baby's large head houses an equally large brain with 10 billion cells, or neurons, at birth—nearly twice as many cells as that of an adult brain. What are not developed in an infant's brain at birth are the synapses, connections between the various brain cells. These connections are formed and shaped by early experiences. It is through these pathways that learning occurs.

The areas in a baby's brain that process sensory information are the first to fully develop. Surely this is not by accident. If you observe how infants gather knowledge by using their senses, you can see why the ability to use these regions of the brain early in their lives is essential and significant.

With this in mind, let's consider the way an infant learns. Looking at the diagram (figure 1) of the immature neuron, we can see how the brain works. For example, a message (which is a pattern of electrical impulses) is received by a neuron in the eyes when the baby sees something. The message travels along the axon (a hairlike fiber that extends from a nerve cell) into the cell body and, in very simple terms, is stored in a dendrite spine. Dendrites are the branchlike processes that extend from the cell body in all directions, increasing its ability to form synapses. As you look at the immature neuron, you will see that there are very few dendrite spines; this is because there has not been very much input yet. But as input increases and a neuron matures, more dendrite spines are formed. These spines are the places where other neurons make connections, or synapses, with this neuron. The basic reason for all of these dendrites is to furnish enough room for the thousands of synapses typically found on a neuron.

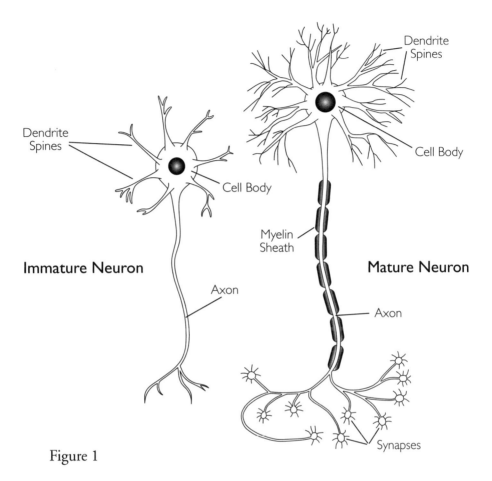

Figure 1

In simplistic terms, every time we learn something, a dendrite spine is formed and the information is stored in this dendrite as a memory. A newborn has virtually no memories, but as the senses start to process sights, smells, touch, tastes, and sounds, information gets processed and memories begin to be stored. It is probably safe to say that one of an infant's first memories is of the mother. But in the brain of the infant, many different dendrites are forming with very specific information about Mom—the sound of her voice, her smell, her smile, her face, the way she picks up the child, and how being held by her feels.

The brain is a mass of neural networks where one memory can trigger another. For example, suppose a good friend calls you on the phone. As soon as you hear her voice, you know who it is. Why? Because you've heard it before and you have this voice stored in your brain, in a dendrite. As you talk, you can visualize her face (stored in another dendrite in a different part of your brain) and then remember various events that you have shared with her (using still other dendrites in completely different parts of your brain). As you talk about what you are having for dinner tonight, you can imagine how it will taste, what it will look like, and so on. Your brain has an infinite capacity to store information and make these neural connections.

Your baby's brain is constantly working to store new information. As neurons are repeatedly used and as they mature, the information travels faster and reactions accelerate. Looking at the mature neuron in the diagram, note the myelin sheath around the axon. This enables messages to travel faster—much as if they were driving on a freeway rather than a dirt road full of potholes. The more ways and opportunities a child has to experience things, the more dendrites will be formed in various parts of the brain, and the chances for more neural connections will increase. When your baby cries or fusses, you ask the question, "Do you want to EAT?" signing the word EAT as you say it. You then offer food. Through the repetition of this simple, everyday event, babies learn that when Mom says EAT and makes that funny hand sign to her mouth, they get food and they get happy. They are able to retrieve this stored information and the neural connection is made. It is just a matter of time.

So what does this mean to the parents of a beautiful, new infant? Generally speaking, the more dendrites there are, the more possible synaptic connections, and the more synaptic connections there are, the better able the neurological system is to process information. Dendrites and synapses are therefore the building blocks of the growth and development of a baby's brain. When activities and experiences are repeated often enough, the dendrites that are used in processing information become permanent and encourage more synaptic growth.

When a baby's knowledge is obtained through the use of multiple senses, even more extensive networks of synapses are formed. The same holds true when particular areas of the brain are actively engaged. For instance, if the language centers are actively involved, more complex patterns of synapses will form in the language region. Such complexity increases the baby's ability to acquire and use language.

Your baby's brain grows fastest during the first two years of life, and your interaction and encouragement will make the most of this window of opportunity. So when you show affection for, talk to, sign with, play with, sing to, laugh with, hold, and touch your baby, know that through your good care and involvement you are helping your child to support and build millions of synapses and dendrites.

Memory

Babies need memory to learn and recall everything around them, from the faces of their family members to the sound of their father's footfall on the steps. As we have seen, the formation of synapses influences and increases memory. Memory is there at birth, and some research indicates that babies can identify their mother's voice through their memory of the prebirth experience in the womb. Memory becomes fully developed by the time they reach school age.

Baby Thoughts

Researchers in the United States and in the United Kingdom have recently disproven the long-held belief that babies do not understand "object permanence"—that is, that a baby's awareness of objects ceases to exist after the object is no longer visible. The U.S. research was conducted at the University of California, Santa Cruz. There, researchers working with 2- and 3-month-old babies discovered that babies as young as 10 weeks old understand object permanence: the babies in the study knew objects continued to exist even when they could no longer see them.

In the United Kingdom study, which took place at Birkbeck College and University College of London, the researchers worked with brain scans to dispel the belief that as far as babies' level of understanding is concerned, when objects are hidden from view they are "out of sight, out of mind." They discovered bursts of brain activity when an object was hidden and again at the time when the baby might expect it to reappear. The researchers believe these activity bursts indicate the baby is thinking about the object when it is not in view.

Both of these studies demonstrate the advanced mental development of very young babies. It is quite amazing to consider the amount and level of comprehension possible in children so early in life. What a wonderful opportunity this offers parents who begin to talk with their babies before they have grown old enough to produce oral speech! With sign language, objects can be identified, people can be named, and ideas can be exchanged.

How Babies Develop

Each baby is unique, a special treasure for us to nurture, guide, support, nourish, and keep safe. All children develop the same and yet differently, as parents of multiple children will tell you. They start to walk and talk at different times and they have different interests and abilities. Yet studies have shown that children develop in many of the same ways and at roughly the same time. Here are some basics on a baby's development.

Visual Input

Vision is perhaps the most critical sense area of a child's development. When you observe an infant, you can see how the eyes are used to explore and examine the surrounding world. More than half of a baby's brain is devoted to visual processing. An interesting new discovery is that babies have a natural ability to notice small differences in intricate visual patterns. Before 3 months of age, infants can recognize a scrambled photograph of their mother just as quickly as a photo in which everything is in the right place.

Eye Gaze

Researcher Andrew Meltzoff, a professor at the University of Washington, has studied the "gaze following" of thousands of babies. He believes that babies learn a good deal about what people are interested in and what they plan to do next by simply watching their eyes. Babies absorb the culture of their community through their eyes.

Eye gaze is an important indicator of a baby's emotional and social growth. It has even been used to predict a child's language development. In Meltzoff's studies, babies who were not proficient at gaze following by their first birthday had much less language development than other children by their second birthday.

You can help your child become more proficient at using eye gaze. By regularly interacting with your infant, pointing out objects, talking, and signing, you will be offering additional gazing opportunities. It is best to do this when the child appears to be settled, quiet, and alert. The baby will be more attentive and responsive to you during such times, and more aware and interested in the surroundings.

Your Baby's Hands

Watch how babies use their hands. You can see how they experiment. They move their hands about; they touch them together; they try to reach things; they attempt to pick up objects. What they learn in this manner is written in the tactile, kinesthetic language of manipulation and movement. It is returned to the brain and compared with the information from the visual system. Through this interaction between the brain and the hand, a kind of dual learning takes place.

Social Interaction

Reaching out to others occurs far earlier than previously understood. Recent research has concluded that babies younger than 6 months of age find specific meaning in people's expressions and are able to distinguish between a smile and a sad face. From birth, they are able to recognize their mother by her voice.

Sign Language and Its Role

So far we have discussed several physiological characteristics shared by babies: the growth of synapses in their brains, the way they rely on visual input, why they use kinesthetic manipulation and movement of the hands to explore their world, and their amazing interest in social interaction during the first months of life. Each of these characteristics offers a strong rationale for using a manual language with a baby.

When these physiological characteristics are examined as a whole, it is easy to understand why signing with babies is becoming more popular every day. You will learn even more reasons to use ASL with your baby in succeeding chapters of this book.

Signing Success Story

Carter began signing when he was about 8 months old. By the time he was 11 months old, he knew and regularly used a few signs. Among them were MORE, ALL DONE, MOMMY, DADDY, HELP, and

LISTEN. One morning when he was sitting in his high chair eating breakfast, Carter started to sign to his mother, Sarah: "LISTEN." "DADDY, LISTEN DADDY." When Sarah listened, she heard his daddy coming down the stairs. Although neither of them could actually see Daddy, Carter had let his mother know that he could hear his Daddy's footsteps on the stairs. From that day forward, Sarah never underestimated how much her little boy knew.

Three Views on Human Development

Three prominent psychologists who deal with child development are important to mention at this time. They are Howard Gardner and his theory of Multiple Intelligences, Erik Erikson with his Stages Theory, and Abraham Maslow and his Hierarchy of Needs. Their studies and theories strongly support the knowledge we have about early learning and child development. You will see how their concepts also support the reasons why signing is such a beneficial activity for babies.

Multiple Intelligences

The need to enhance a child's learning through a varied, multisensory approach has become widely accepted. Howard Gardner says that there is not one specific way to learn and to develop intelligence in children, but multiple ways to do so. Each child does not have fixed intelligence but is developing continuously. Gardner developed a list of Multiple Intelligences, or the multiple ways children learn:

- **Physical (kinesthetic) learning**—movement
- **Verbal learning**—speaking, listening
- **Visual learning**—seeing, reading, pictures
- **Musical learning**—with music, songs, rhythms, melodies

- **Mathematical learning**—by reasoning, problem solving
- **Interpersonal learning**—in groups
- **Intrapersonal learning**—individually
- **Naturalist learning**—from their environment

Children and their developing brains need to be exposed to a rich learning environment that allows them to explore and use as many of these intelligences as possible. Each time a child learns something new or experiences it in a new or different way, new dendrites are formed in various parts of the brain. By combining signing with other activities, such as singing, reading books, using rhymes, conversing, and more, parents and caregivers are not only providing a baby with activities that use a variety of learning styles at the same time, but they are also providing multiple ways to nurture the baby's growing brain.

Building Trust

Erik Erikson, through his studies on human behavior, believed that all people go through various stages of identity development at approximately the same pace. The first stage is called Trust versus Mistrust and involves infants from birth to about 1 year of age. During this stage, infants are learning to trust that their parents and caregivers are going to take care of them and meet their physical needs for nourishment, shelter, and love. Every time you answer a cry, change a diaper, take care of a need, feed, bathe, rock, comfort, cuddle, talk to, sing to, or play with your baby, you are sending the infant the message that your baby is being taken care of, being loved, and can trust you. If, however, the child's needs are not met but instead are neglected or met with indifference, the child feels mistrust and feels unloved.

Although this section offers merely a snapshot of these theorists and their theories, these concepts are significant to the whole picture. If you can understand how to meet your baby's needs because there is communication with you, it is a win-win situation. Signing offers you this opportunity.

Hierarchy of Needs

To explain the Hierarchy of Needs, Abraham Maslow used a pyramid to show how people all have the same basic need structure. At the base or foundation of this hierarchy (see figure 2) is what he calls the Physical Needs. All the other needs are built on this one. If infants are fed, clothed, and sheltered, if they are warm, clean, and cared for—if their basic, physical needs

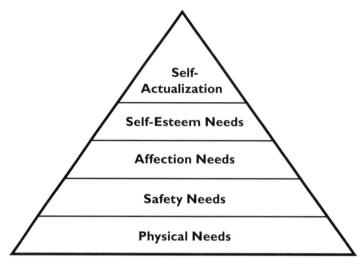

Maslow's Hierarchy of Needs
As you grow and your physical needs are taken care of, you
seek to satisfy other needs on the pyramid:
• Safety Needs—to know that you are safe
• Affection Needs—to know that someone cares about you
• Self-Esteem Needs—to know that you are doing a good job
• Self-Actualization—to reach your potential

Figure 2

are being met—they are, for the most part, content. This is what parents do
all day—meet their babies' physical needs and wants. This is why signing is so
wonderful. When babies can tell us what they need, it helps us to meet and
satisfy these needs.

Conclusion

As you can see, signing is an amazing and beneficial activity for babies,
their parents, and their caregivers. It fits so well with our knowledge of a baby's
developmental process. Signing encourages brain development and helps to
foster memory retention. It allows babies to communicate thoughts that they
cannot verbally communicate yet. It lets babies satisfy some of their basic
physical needs without crying. It encourages social interaction that supports
trust, love, and bonding. It allows babies to use a wide variety of learning styles
simultaneously. Signing is not a current fad but a real language and learning
skill that has proven benefits for all babies.

Chapter 3
The Power of Language

As an adult, you undoubtedly do not think about your spoken language very often. It has been a part of your world for such a long time that you have come to take it for granted. However, if you travel to a foreign country and encounter expressions and words you do not know, you become keenly aware of how much we rely on language.

When you are able to name something, on some level you feel you control it. If you are shopping in a produce market and are able to recognize and name the various items, you feel knowledgeable and comfortable as well. It is confusing to encounter a fruit or vegetable that you cannot identify.

If you are searching for an unfamiliar item for a new recipe and cannot locate it in the store, you will have to resort to asking the greengrocer where to find it. After you learn what this fruit or vegetable looks like, you will often begin to notice it in several other places. This may be surprising to you. You have discovered its shape, size, and color, and you can name it. Because you can visually identify this fruit or vegetable and you know the word we use to signify it, the produce has a heightened relevance in your life.

This analogy illustrates what is happening to babies as they begin exploring the world, which is a foreign country to them. Everything is new and full of surprises, and they have no language to express or codify this experience.

The Origins of Language

Today the general consensus among researchers interested in the origins of spoken language is that all human languages must have evolved from manual communication to vocalization. This is not a new idea. The 18th century French philosopher Etienne Condillac believed that human language did not begin with vocalization but evolved from gesture to speech. When you think about it, this understanding makes sense because gestures, and their iconic nature, easily illustrate the shape and position of objects or actions in space.

In the development of human beings, sign and gesture appear to have predated speech. Michael C. Corballis explores this concept in his article "The Gestural Origins of Language," published in *American Scientist*.[1] He points out that if the earliest languages were gestural, this would explain how words arbitrarily came to represent objects and actions: "What may have begun as an iconic system could plausibly have evolved more abstract properties over time, and at some point arbitrary patterns of sound may have been linked to gestures that may themselves have become abstract symbols rather than icons."[2]

Why is it important for parents who are teaching their infants sign language to understand the source of language? If, as all the current evidence indicates, the first way that human beings communicated was with their hands, then babies undoubtedly have a capacity to use this mode of communication. Signing most likely feels as natural or comfortable to a baby as suckling, because not only do babies possess the necessary physical attributes to begin to form signs, but they may well have an innate predisposition to this form of communication.

The Preverbal Period

During the preverbal period of the baby's life, various elements in the baby's social perception are coming into play. There are developmental factors behind the infant's early fascination with and exploration of objects. Infants begin to use their hands and fingers to manipulate objects and point them out to others. This is what Katherine Nelson referred to as a coordination of the social and object worlds.[3] This activity prepares babies for communication using symbols.

Their responsiveness to parents and caregivers is also developing. Studies have shown that infants' first attempts at communication usually involve gesture or eye gaze, often in a situation where both the adult and the child are paying attention to the same object. This early object sharing supports the babies' transition to symbolic communication.[4]

In the preverbal period of hearing babies, the interaction between mother and child is crucial. It becomes the foundation on which the child first gains the ability to communicate and then to use language. The time you spend interacting with your child gives the baby multiple opportunities to begin to communicate, beginning with reaching, giving, showing, or pointing gestures.

Early Signing

There are many differences between a baby learning a signed language, such as ASL, and learning a spoken language, such as English. For one, an infant can begin to master a signed language at a much earlier age. Babies are capable of signing well before they have the physical ability to begin to speak.

The first 6 months of infants' gestures were systematically studied by Alan Fogel, who discovered that the hand configurations that occur most frequently in young children's initial signing vocabularies are typically produced by all children during their first 6 months.[5] It is thus quite plausible that babies can begin to make recognizable signs at a very young age.

Cowlyn Trevarthen found that many of the hand movements involved in the adult gestures of pointing, waving, reaching, and grasping appear in babies as early as the first few months of life.[6] Trevarthen, as well as other scholars, stresses the social foundation of all language learning in infancy. Babies are interested in communicating with their caregivers, and they are able to physically form the hand configurations and movements of a visual-gestural language such as ASL well before they are able to produce the sounds of an oral language .

Imitating Movements

Since the middle of the 20th century, when the Swiss psychologist Jean Piaget won world fame for his studies of the thought processes of children, we have known that babies develop motor imitation skills early in their first year. Piaget believed that children pass through four periods of intellectual development.[7] Of these, the period that is relevant for babies is his first period, the sensorimotor period, which extends from birth to about 2 years of age. The second period, the preoperational period, occurs from 2 to 7 years of age. The third period, called the period of concrete operations, and the final stage, the period of formal operations, occur when children are older.

During the sensorimotor period, children obtain a basic understanding of their world through their senses. In the fourth phase of the sensorimotor period, which occurs when a child is 8 to 12 months old, infants are quite successful at imitating other people's movements.[8]

According to Barbara Schaeffer, because babies are born with an inherent ability to imitate movements, they are particularly adept at learning a manual language.[9] Schaeffer found that learning signs at an early age can actually help babies develop the interactional skills necessary for language learning in any form. These are skills like seeking eye contact, imitating gestures, or touching an adult to get attention. All of these attributes are prerequisites of learning an oral language.

Learning to Speak

Nature provides children with the ability to acquire an oral language. And it is not happenstance that all of the children in this world will acquire the language of the place where they are reared from the language users around them. They will do this naturally, spontaneously, and without any specific effort or instruction. By listening to others during the early years of their lives, children learn their native language in a fairly orderly way. By the time they are 6 years old, they will possess and understand the grammar of their native language.

Babies are physically unable to make speechlike sounds until they are between 1 and 2 years old. This is because a baby's larynx, the top part of the trachea, sticks up in the back of the throat when the baby is born. This allows the baby to suckle and breathe at the same time.

The larynx must drop at least 3 centimeters before it becomes the voice box and can produce speechlike sounds. This gradually happens during the first 18 to 24 months of a child's life. Generally, by the time a baby is 2 years old the larynx has descended to a position at the C3 vertebra, and the baby has the physical ability to produce speech sounds. The larynx will continue to descend, and by the time a child is 6 years old it will have reached its adult site, between the C4 and C7 vertebrae.[10]

Intelligible Speech

Intelligible speech does not usually occur until a child is close to 2 years of age. Speech sounds are formed in the mouth after the air produced by the lungs passes over the vocal folds found in the larynx. What transpires in the mouth to create the sounds we understand as intelligible speech?

Moving air is formed into the sounds of words by the articulators located in the mouth. These articulators are the gum ridge, the teeth, the tongue, and the soft and hard palates. Most of these articulators mature gradually as the child develops during the first four years of life. Therefore, truly intelligible speech is not possible for most children until that age.

Keep in mind that all physiological development arrives at various times for different children. The ages given here are maturation averages. All of us did not gain the ability to sit up, walk, or skip at the same age. Likewise, all children do not acquire the ability to speak at exactly the same age. There is a typical range during which the speech apparatus develops to a degree that permits a young child to form intelligible words and begin to communicate with spoken language.

Using Hands to Communicate

From the time they are born, all typically developing babies, whether they are deaf or hearing, use their hands to explore their environment. They examine objects, reach, and grasp. Some suck their fingers. Deaf or hearing infants, in homes where they are exposed to sign language, learn to use their hands to communicate their feelings and desires. They generally begin to use sign language when they are about 6 months old.

Before hearing children begin to speak, the only mode of communication available to them is crying or whining. As we have seen, babies remain physiologically unable to produce discernible oral language until they are about 18 months of age. While they remain without a mechanism to produce such language, babies who are exposed to a sign language have the physical ability to form signs and communicate with their hands for almost a full year before nonsigning babies begin to use language. In most cases, nonsigning babies do not use their hands to produce language until they begin to print.

Why does this matter? Because there is a physiological advantage in using the hands to produce language. During the 19th century, the Scottish surgeon and anatomy teacher Sir Charles Bell stressed the interconnected relationship among movement, perception, and learning. Bell's research examined the interdependence of hand and brain function.

According to Bell, both the hand and eye develop as sense organs through practice. The brain teaches itself by making the hand and eye learn together. The brain constructs images based on the messages received from the eye and hand. It records a collection of sensory data derived from the eye and limb movements.

Current Research

Contemporary research bears out and strengthens Bell's assertions about how the coupling of hand and eye movements relates to the development of thought and language development. Frank R. Wilson, a neurologist at the University of California School of Medicine in San Francisco, writes in *The Hand: How Its Use Shapes the Brain, Language, and Human Culture* that a great deal of evidence indicates that the link between thought and language development is the hand-thought-language connection.[11] Wilson explains that a child learns with real objects unified through a sequence of actions organizing his or her active movements and sensorimotor explorations.

Wilson stresses that "none of the neurophysiological brain activity can be related to real language until it gains access to an input-output channel."[12] This is important for our discussion because most children use oral language as an "input-output channel"—in other words, as a way to communicate. Signing children have access to another way to communicate that is suited for their use. Because children are capable of using sign language at a much younger age than they can use spoken language, signing children have access to an input-output channel much sooner.

When connections among interwoven strands of language and thought are created with sign language, language and thought are intrinsically attached to what is happening to the child's hand. As the brain learns to send and receive coded messages, language milestones occur at the same time as motor milestones, developing on parallel tracks but always interconnected, interdependent, growing, reinforcing, and influencing each other. The hand is the biomechanical link found at the end (or the beginning, depending on your perspective) of an elaborate, enormously complex physical and mental circuit.[13]

Babies' Feelings

Today our understanding of a baby's ability in this realm is changing. The factual information in this chapter will help you understand why identifying and labeling emotions can be a huge benefit for your baby. You can find out more about this in chapter 7.

Recent research demonstrates that babies who are not yet able to utter an intelligible syllable can feel and express complex emotions such as envy or jealousy. In one such study, conducted at Texas Tech University, researchers observed the reactions of 6-month-old infants when their mothers appeared to be caring for another baby. A baby was placed in an infant seat next to the mother's chair. A researcher placed a lifelike doll in the mother's arms, and the mother proceeded to rock and pay attention to the baby doll. When this occurred, the baby began to cry and carry on, as if in physical distress. Consumed with jealousy, the tiny baby forcefully and loudly expressed this feeling. All the babies in the study had a similar reaction when they believed their mom was caring for another baby and paying little attention to them.

Another study, at the University of Minnesota, was able to show through brain activity that babies who could not even sit up yet could identify or distinguish among several emotional facial expressions. Much of this recent research shows that babies feel and understand complicated emotions such as empathy, surprise, and frustration.

How do these findings relate to the development and education of your baby? Helping your child identify emotions and label each of them with an appropriate ASL sign and English word offers the child an opportunity to begin to comprehend these feelings more fully. This opens a much earlier pathway for you to help your child to recognize a variety of feelings and learn to respond or react to them in a positive manner. Achieving and enjoying an emotional equilibrium at a younger age ensures a more pleasant babyhood and toddler time for your child—and for you.

Communication: The Heart of Our Humanness

Communication is at the very heart of our humanity. A baby who is able to communicate at an early age is likely to gain both an emotional and an educational advantage. For all the previously cited reasons, signing with an infant is an adventure that brings immediate pleasure to both the caregiver and the child. As the two of you begin to use this manual language to share knowledge and feelings, a rich emotional relationship will emerge. Through this communication channel, your baby will be able to acquire information and begin to develop a deeper, fuller relationship with you.

Signing Success Story

From the time Amber was 6 months old, her mother began to sign with her, starting with signs like MORE, EAT, ALL DONE, and BOTTLE. As time went on she began to add more words, especially when reading books to Amber. Amber really loved animal books and one of her favorite animals was a MONKEY. Her mother learned the sign for monkey and used it as often as she could.

One day when Amber was just a little over 12 months old, her father was reading books with her. They came upon a picture of a monkey. Amber signed MONKEY and made monkey sounds. Her dad realized right away that she was making a sign, and from the look of it and the sounds she was making it had to be a monkey. He praised Amber for her efforts. He then decided to read a new book, but Amber would have no part of it. She wanted the monkey book again and again.

As time went on, Amber began to sign many more animals, and her dad had to become much more aware of the signs she was learning so that he could understand them when he saw them.

Conclusion

You and your baby will communicate with signing because it is a manual language that is not only at the heart of our human heritage but is also a language that babies are physically capable of using. The hand control needed to sign develops earlier than oral skills, and the use of sign language will enhance language development. Signing is a powerful activity that has positive influences on babies and children of all ages.

Mothers have come to realize that signing activities augment their babies' language connection. By combining spoken words with ASL, babies hear words, see words, feel words, and spend time engaged with their parents. The results demonstrate that babies and children develop larger vocabularies and greater language skills through signing.

Chapter 4
Why Use ASL?

American Sign Language is the unvoiced language used by members of the Deaf community. It is a popular and modern language that is commonly used in the United States. In addition to fulfilling foreign or modern language requirements in high schools and colleges, ASL is being used to encourage early communication in hearing babies, as well as to promote literacy in early childhood education.

All of these facts were not always true about ASL. This chapter will cover why ASL is a popular language today and relate some of its history. It will clarify the reasons why all Sign to Speak materials recommend ASL signs rather than signs that you might make up yourself.

The Origins of Sign Language

Deaf people have always communicated with signs formed by their hands. Research shows that babies who are deaf will babble with their hands in much the same way that hearing babies babble with their voices. Both are natural precursors to the manual or oral language that will follow. So the actual origins of a signed language can be found within Deaf communities.

Deaf Populations in the United States

When groups of deaf people live in a specific region, a signed language emerges. This occurred during the 18th and 19th centuries on Martha's Vineyard, a small island off the Massachusetts coast. The existence of a recessive gene caused a specific form of deafness to frequently occur within this isolated population. At the peak of the incidence of deafness on the island, one in every four babies born was deaf. Sign language became so prevalent on the Vineyard that everybody used it, and both hearing and deaf individuals became equally adept at talking with their hands.

During the early 19th century the United States was experiencing a surge in philanthropy, providing individuals considered unfortunate with needed support. A group of Connecticut benefactors led by Mason Cogswell, who himself had a daughter that was deaf, were interested in providing education for the young deaf population of New England. Based on evidence gathered at the time, there were about 400 prospective students. Thomas Hopkins Gallaudet, Cogswell's neighbor and a young Yale graduate, was sent to Europe to observe and learn the methods used for teaching in European schools for the Deaf. Gallaudet's goal was to bring this education to the United States.

French Sign Language

After first unsuccessfully exploring what the United Kingdom had to offer, Gallaudet was welcomed at the French School for the Deaf. He was captivated by two deaf young teachers at the Paris school, Jean Massieu and Laurent Clerc. Gallaudet watched them teach and took classes from them. He was impressed with the breadth of their knowledge and depth of their understanding. Massieu's description of the meaning of the word *gratitude* as "memory of the heart" charmed him. Gallaudet proposed that Clerc come to the United States and serve as a teacher in the school he intended to establish. After gaining permission from Abbé Sicard, the principal of the school, and sadly bidding his mother good-bye, Clerc joined Gallaudet on his journey across the ocean.

During the voyage, Gallaudet taught Clerc English, and Clerc taught Gallaudet sign language and the manual alphabet. This alphabet, a one-handed way to signify every letter in the written alphabet, is an integral part of the language and is used to spell words. The sign language that Clerc taught Gallaudet was French Sign Language (FSL). This was the indigenous sign language of French natives coupled with methodical markers introduced by the Abbé de l'Epée, who in 1755 had founded the world's first public school for children who were deaf. As a parish priest, de l'Epée had encountered children in the Deaf community using signs. He learned their language and used it to teach them to read and write French.

The American School for the Deaf

Clerc and Gallaudet landed in the United States on August 9, 1816, and opened their school on August 15, 1817, with Gallaudet as the principal and Clerc as the head teacher. It was the first school for the Deaf in the nation. As it grew, this school would move to three locations in the Hartford, Connecticut, area. Today, it is called the American School for the Deaf and is known as the mother school of 64 similar schools in this country.

A large number of the earl[...] [...] Vineyard. Others, who came fro[...] using what were commonly kn[...] originated within the homes of [...] the Deaf person and shared with[...] systems and is similar to the diffe[...] English in spoken language. Thes[...] the French Sign Language used b[...] signing that would eventually be[...]

Love and Marriage

Clerc and Gallaudet each fe[...] the school. Both of these your[...] become significant contributors[...] of sign language within it.

Sophia Fowler, Gallaudet's wife, became the mother of eight children, all of whom were native signers. In 1857, her youngest son, Edward Miner Gallaudet, founded the institution now known as Gallaudet University in Washington DC. She joined Edward in Washington and served as matron of the fledgling school. At the time she was in her 60s, her 20-year-old son wrote that he believed she gave an air of dignity and distinction to the establishment. His mother was always the model for him of what a Deaf person could accomplish. He found the sign language they had always used for communication to be a rich and rewarding language that was every bit as capable of encoding abstract ideas as English.

Sign language was always the language used for instruction at the American School, and it continued as the language for instruction at the Washington institution under the direction of Edward Miner Gallaudet. The majority of instructors in both schools were Deaf, and the students flourished academically during this early period with its strong sign language focus. Their Deaf instructors used sign language to teach their courses and taught English only as a written language. There was never confusion between language and speech because speech was not equated with language. The students could read, write, and understand English and also use sign language to communicate. They knew two languages, English and sign language.

Dark Days for Sign Language

In 1880, at the International Congress of Instructors of the Deaf held in Milan, Italy, a serious blow was dealt to the future of the language that would come to be known as ASL. At this conference a vote was taken, and a majority of the attendees, who were proponents of oralism, cast votes in favor of teaching articulation and lipreading and eliminating all instruction in sign language. Oralism refers to the attempt to teach Deaf individuals to understand and use the spoken language of their countries.

Sign language entered a dark period with an uncertain future. For the next 80 years signing was mainly combined with spoken English in a variety of methods and some schools even opted for a strictly oral approach—many were named oral schools for the Deaf. This would be akin to having seeing schools for the blind. Edward Miner Gallaudet and those administrators and teachers who followed him at Gallaudet University always made a place for sign language on the campus. Indeed, it was at Gallaudet University in the 1960s when sign language would again come into prominence with the seminal work of William Stokoe, one of the school's English professors.

The Language of ASL

William Stokoe was familiar with the sign language the students were using on campus, and he studied the signing more closely in his language laboratory tucked away in the university basement. He published his groundbreaking book *Sign Language Structure* in 1960, demonstrating that sign language was indeed a complete independent language with all the hallmarks of any language. The initial reaction to his endeavors was lukewarm. However, his ideas were gradually accepted and adopted.

Stokoe has become world famous for his research and is recognized as the primary person responsible for identifying the true nature of American Sign Language. Because he realized that the intricate movements of his students' hands and bodies represented a fully developed language that met all linguistic criteria, he is often identified as the Father of American Sign Language. Surprisingly, Dr. Stokoe did not see the full language legitimacy he and those who followed him bestowed on ASL as his greatest accomplishment. Rather, he explains, "What I consider my principal discovery is how language must have begun as Sign. That is to say briefly: an upright walking visually oriented, late evolving primary species began to see that body movements really did mean what they looked as if they meant. Voice can make sound but the only way that a wealth of meanings can be connected to sounds is by being told what the sounds mean. If gestures had developed into actual language—and much sign research shows they have done so—then sounds habitually uttered along with gestures would have become connected with meanings that the gestures had naturally signified."[1]

Ultimately, other linguists supported Stokoe's view and recognized ASL as a true language. With this understanding of it as an actual, complete, albeit unvoiced, language, ASL began to receive acceptance in a wider venue. It was used to fulfill modern or foreign language requirements, first in colleges and universities and soon in high schools. Since 1987, ASL has fulfilled foreign language requirements in California high schools. It is now accepted as a modern language in virtually all states and is taught as such in many secondary schools.

Dr. Stokoe devoted the last years of his life to conducting additional research that would further anchor his beliefs. He diligently worked on his manuscript during his final illness. Further findings of what Dr. Stokoe considered to be his principal discovery—that human language began as sign language—can be found in his posthumously published book *Language in Hand: Why Sign Came Before Speech.*

In this book, Stokoe makes the point that sounds can do many things, such as frighten, startle, or beckon, but unless they are aided by convention they cannot represent nounlike or verblike concepts. They are powerless to show even a rudimentary relationship to meaning. Sounds can be linked to word and sentence meanings only by standard usage.[2]

Stokoe finds that humans gain a clear understanding of movement, and are aware that movement toward self differs from movement away from self, at an early age. He asserts that this idea is crucial to understanding the meanings of signs. He observes that infants acquire this knowledge when they move their hands and arms and manipulate objects in the world around them. Viewing or feeling the direction of physical actions is simple and obvious. Visible movements have carried meaning for millions of years. Therefore, Stokoe concludes, a gestural, visual language is the most likely candidate for the first language.[3]

ASL as a Teaching Tool

At the same time ASL was gaining recognition and use as an authentic language, educators were appropriating it as a teaching tool. It had been used in the 1960s and 1970s with special-needs students as a communication device, mainly for nonverbal students. In the 1980s and 1990s, sign found its way into mainstream education for typical hearing students. Preschool and kindergarten teachers discovered ASL. The manual alphabet helped their students recognize letters and words, and benefited their literacy development.

In this book we use the same manual alphabet and signs for concepts and words as the Deaf community, but we do not use the syntax or word order of ASL. Instead, we use what is called Contact Signing, the combination of ASL signs and concepts with spoken English word order, since your primary purpose for using ASL is to facilitate your baby's comprehension and use of the English language.

ASL word order is quite different from English word order. In general, ASL word order is the reverse of English, where we place the descriptor before the object, as in a white house, or a large brown leather chair, and so on. In ASL the order would be house white and chair leather brown large. ASL also uses a particular order to describe others. The gender is always first, followed by height, body type, color of hair, and hairstyle.

The Advantages of ASL

Thomas Hopkins Gallaudet found that sign language had many advantages. He thought the meanings of words were more easily understood in sign and that forming the manual alphabet would aid in remembering words and their spellings. He believed it was good for hearing siblings of the students of the American School to learn sign language, not only to enable them to communicate with their sisters and brothers but for their own benefit. Gallaudet was certain that the more varied the forms of language, whether voiced or manual, the better it would be understood and recalled by children.

Nearly 200 years after Gallaudet set forth his beliefs about the multiple benefits of sign language, current research and our newest technologies are providing support for his insights. Marilyn's research demonstrates the enhanced spelling ability of students who use the manual alphabet as a spelling aid. More than a dozen of her published works show that when you use sign language with children, they will have a 20 percent larger receptive English vocabulary.

ASL for Hearing Babies

Soon after ASL began to appear regularly in educational institutions for use with young children, it found its way into homes. Some mothers were introduced to sign language by their toddlers, their preschoolers, or their children's preschool teachers. Other moms knew ASL because they had learned it as a language in school. Books were published that touted the benefits of sign for infants, videotapes and DVDs followed, and by the first decade of the 21st century, signing with babies was an idea whose time had come.

Today, many moms are using ASL to facilitate earlier communication with their infants. They realize the multiple advantages exposure to this unvoiced language offers a baby. Signing involves movement, a key component to childhood learning. It develops eye-hand coordination, along with fine motor skills. Signs are easy to form and are often recognizable because they are often iconic, meaning they actually look like the thing or action they represent.

By using ASL, babies and children are exposed to a second language. ASL signs are consistent, and through them, children learn words that are used all across the United States and in a variety of life's experiences. They can meet other children and adults who use sign—at school, on vacation, at church, and even while playing. They see ASL signed at sporting events, concerts, and on television. By learning ASL vocabulary, children and parents are opening up opportunities in their lives to begin communicating and interacting with the Deaf community.

Signing Success Story

When Matthew was about 14 months old, he went to his family's annual Christmas Eve party. This was the first real Christmas party where he was aware of what was going on, and he was very excited about all the activities. At these parties, all the children get to play rhythm instruments (such as bells and shakers) and sing Christmas songs with their parents, cousins, and many friends. The first song of the night was "Jingle Bells." Matthew was mesmerized by the singing, guitar playing, and all the sounds the other children were making. When the song was over, he walked up to his grandpa, who was playing the guitar and leading the group, and began to excitedly sign MORE, MORE, MORE. His grandfather recognized the sign and, of course, did exactly what Matthew wanted: he began to play, and everyone sang more and more songs.

Why Not Use Made-Up Signs and Gestures?

There are five great reasons for using American Sign Language instead of made-up signs and gestures.

1. ASL is a structured language, with vocabulary that exists and dictionaries you can access for existing signs.

2. It is one of the most common languages in the United States, so by teaching ASL vocabulary you are giving your baby the foundation for learning a "real" second language.

3. American Sign Language is recognized and spoken by millions of people across the United States whereas made-up gestures are generally understood only by family members.

4. It is taught in preschools and schools across the country. When children encounter it, they will already have knowledge of and vocabulary for ASL that is in common with other children.

5. ASL allows children to interact with Deaf children and the Deaf community.

Conclusion

Parents and caregivers are offered a variety of choices for signing with their babies. Our view is that American Sign Language vocabulary is the preferred method in regard to the use of signs with babies. ASL is a major language in the United States, having a structure and vocabulary, and it is well established. By using ASL, you are introducing a second language that exists right alongside spoken English. It is universal and is spoken and recognized by millions of people.

ASL keeps things simple. It standardizes the words you will be using and provides you with dictionaries and other resources to develop signs that are of interest to you and your baby. And, unlike with made-up signs, if you forget a word, you can just look it up. Finally, as your baby grows into other childhood stages, ASL can continue to provide the same benefits to communication and language development into elementary school.

PART 2
How to Sign with Your Baby

Chapter 5
Get a Jump Start on Smart

This chapter is designed to get you started signing with your baby right now. You don't need to know a single sign to begin; all you need is the desire and a few effective signs and tips to help you. Because of our signing experience, you can be sure that the information and signs we are providing will allow you to be successful at incorporating sign into your and your baby's lives.

This chapter will get you started signing right now! You will learn three of the most popular and successfully used signs with babies. Once you become comfortable with these Jump Start signs, move on to chapter 7, where you will find additional signs that are effective with babies. You can also, at any time, begin to add the activities we have provided in part 3 of the book. The games, songs, rhymes, and more will increase your usable sign vocabulary in a fun, interactive way. Keep in mind that we are giving you an outline for signing. Choose our plan or adapt it to fit your needs and desires.

Start Signing Right Now!

If you are like most people who want to begin using sign, you probably don't know many, if any, American Sign Language words. The three signs we are offering here have proven over the years to be highly effective because they go to the heart of communicating a baby's basic wants and needs. By learning these and then following a few simple rules, you'll be on your way.

We know that babies understand words. We know that a manual language, in our case ASL, facilitates communication for them. As we discussed in part 1, this is because babies develop the ability to control their hands far sooner than the muscles of their vocal apparatus (mouth, tongue, and throat) needed to speak. When we use sign language with babies and children, we offer them the gift of language.

The First Three Signs

One of Ken and Georgia's daughters believes that it takes only the three Jump Start on Smart signs to be successful with early communication. She had grown up around signing, and when she had her first child she began to use signs with him when he was about 3 months old. When her son was about 18 months old, she went to Ken and said, "Dad, how do people raise children without signing EAT, MORE, and ALL DONE? These signs have made my life so much easier." These three signs have made thousands of parents' lives easier.

EAT, ALL DONE, and MORE are the first three signs we suggest parents use with babies. For many parents, keeping it simple and signing a few words, then adding more when you see that your baby is ready, is an effective approach to signing. Let's get started with our Jump Start on Smart signs, which really go to communicating a baby's basic wants and needs.

EAT

For many years, the number-one word parents and caregivers have asked us to teach them is EAT. This word goes right to the core of communication.

It is especially effective when taught and used consistently at meal time. You can ask your baby and sign the word, "Would you like to EAT cereal? Do you want to EAT some banana?"

EAT—Hold the fingertips of one hand together and bring your hand up to your mouth repeatedly (as if you are eating something).

ALL DONE

For many parents, the sign for ALL DONE, which is also used for the word finished, is another effective sign. You can use ALL DONE in so many ways: for example, "Are you ALL DONE eating?" or "Are we ALL DONE walking?" Babies often come to embrace this word and use it for anything they want to stop doing.

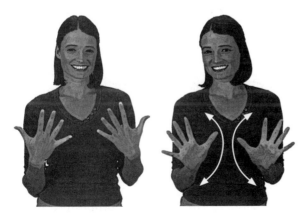

ALL DONE / FINISHED— Hold up both hands with palms in, fingers at chest level, with palms flat and fingers loose. Then, in a quick motion, turn your palms so that they are facing down, fingers are forward. Repeat.

MORE

Next is the sign for MORE. MORE is a wonderful sign that you can teach your child in so many different and creative ways. You can ask, "Would you like MORE to EAT?" and sign both MORE and EAT in a combination. "MORE milk? MORE swinging? Do you want MORE, or are you ALL DONE?" Anytime you get the chance to use the word and have your baby's attention, sign and say the word MORE.

MORE—Hold the fingertips of both hands together (as you do with one hand for EAT) and then tap them together. Repeat.

"Keep It Simple" Rules for Signing with Babies

Here are "Keep It Simple" rules to keep in mind. By following these rules, you will find that signing is not complicated. It will fit easily into your everyday life and give your child the gift of early language.

- **Get your baby's attention.** One of the best ways to do this is to sign at meaningful times, such as meal time, bath time, story time, playtime, or song time.
- **Be consistent.** Use the correct ASL sign every time you say the word.
- **Enunciate words and sign clearly.** Speak and sign together.
- **Repeat spoken and signed words often.** Providing multiple opportunities each day for your baby to hear and see signed words.
- **Keep signing simple.** Begin with only a few signs. Add more signs as you become more comfortable with the signs you know and when you begin to see your baby signing back.

- **Be patient.** Generally the younger the baby, the longer it will be until you see your baby signing back. Babies vary, but most will begin to sign words sometime between 9 and 14 months.
- **Be creative.** Create signing opportunities each day so that you use your signs as often as you can. For repetition, you can use the signs in playful activities such as reading or singing.
- **Reinforce the learning of signs.** Connect signs and their meaning to yourself or others, as in "Mommy's ALL DONE!" or "Daddy wants MORE, too!"

Signing Success Story

Jimmy's mom started signing with him when he was about 6 months old. By the time he was 12 months old, she had a collection of about 12 signs that she was consistently using with him, but he had not yet begun to sign back to her. One afternoon, she had to go to the store and took Jimmy with her. He hated to go for rides in the car. When she put him in his car seat and began to buckle him in, she was excited to see Jimmy frantically signing ALL DONE, ALL DONE, ALL DONE! He wasn't crying or screaming, but he was certainly signing with enthusiasm. His signing didn't get him out of the car ride, but from that day on, signing just seemed to blossom. By 16 months old he had a vocabulary of about 20 signs in addition to his spoken words.

Conclusion

Keep on signing. We have offered you three signs for getting started: EAT, ALL DONE, and MORE. In later chapters we will be offering you many more signs to use. Start out at your own pace, adding signs when you are ready.

Activities with signing help both you and your baby learn to use signs. Whatever signs you add, make it a routine to sign the word every time you say it. Be sure you have your baby's attention. Enjoy the excitement you feel when your baby begins to sign words to you.

Chapter 6
Master the Basics

Though signing is not a difficult activity to do with your baby, you probably have a variety of questions about it: When is a good time to start signing? How much do I need to know? And what else do I need to do in order to be successful? This chapter will answer those questions as well as provide you with more signing information and basic rules. When you put all these elements together, they will ensure your success when signing with your baby.

Are You and Your Baby Ready?

Many parents want to know when their babies are ready to start signing. This depends on the baby—and on you.

Your Baby

Is your baby happy and content? Does your baby appear ready to learn? Is your baby watching you intently? If the answer to all these questions is yes, then your child is ready to begin to learn signs. If, on the other hand, your baby is distracted or not paying attention, then it is best to wait until these issues have been resolved before introducing signing. When both you and your baby are at ease, signing will be comfortable, fun, and an activity to anticipate and engage in with pleasure.

You

Furthermore, it is not just your personality or your baby's demeanor or apparent interest in socialization that should be the deciding factor in determining when to introduce signs in your baby's daily routine. Today's parents have many obligations. Sometimes the demands of a job, or additional pressing family responsibilities, will not permit you to devote the kind of time and effort to signing that you would like. When such distractions exist, it is best to wait until the time of stress has passed. Then you can begin to use sign with your baby in comfort and ease.

Your Baby's Signing

How will your baby relate to signing? Most babies take easily to signing. Signing is a natural activity for them. They are physiologically set to use their eyes and hands to respond to, explore, and learn about the world.

Signing allows you to take advantage of babies' natural desire to be social and interact with others. It connects with their ability to use their hands at an early age and will allow them to develop many more words—both signed and spoken—than nonsigning children.

When to Start

When is the best time to start? How old should your baby be? What sign words should you begin with? The answers to these questions vary from educator to educator. As the parent, you have an opportunity to make your own decision. Here are the facts: Infants with a Deaf signing parent are the earliest signers. The babies of interpreters come in second, and children of hearing parents are third. The reason sign language is acquired by these three groups of babies in this order may be connected with the time signing is initiated with a baby.

Three Alternatives

Deaf parents sign with their babies from birth. Interpreters begin to sign with their babies at about 3 months of age. Hearing parents tend to begin signing with their babies at about 6 months of age. But you must keep in mind that signing is not a race. Sign language will prove to be a benefit for your baby at whatever age you choose to begin.

A Reason to Start Early

Starting earlier will give you a greater opportunity to become familiar with signing. You will have more practice integrating ASL with your spoken words. Before long, it should become second nature to you to simultaneously sign and speak. When signing begins to feel natural and you do not have to think about it, you can focus more of your attention on the baby. It will be easier for you to recognize your baby's early attempts at signing.

There may be a correlation between when you begin signing and when your baby begins to sign. It is logical to believe that starting earlier will produce quicker results. Early signing may create a heightened awareness of your baby's early attempts to sign, and the praise you offer encourages more signing. Through early signing, your child will be communicating with you at a younger age.

A Reason to Wait

Some educators fear that if a parent starts to sign when the baby is quite young, the baby may not begin to sign as soon as the parent would like. The parent might become frustrated and want to give up signing. Some parents may not have the patience to continue to engage their baby with signs over a long period of time without receiving returning signs from the baby.

You Decide

Marilyn's position is that it is never too early to begin and never too late to start. Given what is known now, it is truly up to you. No definitive evidence exists that one time is better than another, or that sooner is better than later. Each parent is different and each baby is different. Some people have a great deal of patience; they will stick to an exercise program or make entries in a journal every day. Others will give up yoga or running after a short period of time, and after a few weeks will not even remember where they put their journal. You know which type of person you are, so you will be able to make the best decision concerning the time to start signing with your baby. Follow the simple steps in this book. Once you begin, be creative and have fun, but be consistent. Anyone can do it!

Is It Hard to Sign?

How will you relate to signing? How soon will you feel comfortable doing it? This varies from person to person. We each have different strengths and enjoy different activities. Some of us love to sing and often will sing with our children. Other parents are keen on reading and will read to their baby before the baby can even understand the words.

It is much the same with signing. Because of its physical nature, some parents will find it easy to recall and form the signs. It will be almost second nature. Others will need to devote more energy to recalling and forming the signs. Ultimately, the key to your success is your desire to sign with your baby. Most parents come to acquire a good feeling about signing after about a month of using signs with their baby. They will become even more enthusiastic when the baby begins to sign. It is a grand day indeed when you and your baby are actually communicating with each other in sign language.

Your Signing Skills

To be successful at signing with your baby, all you need is the desire to incorporate this engaging activity into your daily life. Sometimes parents believe they need previous signing skills. This is not necessary. You will be able to learn the ASL signs; they are uncomplicated and fun. They often look like the word you are saying. You and your baby can learn them together. All you need is a desire to enhance your child's cognitive growth and development. Your commitment and enthusiasm will go a long way toward ensuring success for both you and your infant.

How Many Signs Do You Need to Learn?

How many signs should you use? Can you use too few? Can you use too many? Again, educators have different views. Deaf parents constantly sign with their hearing offspring. They use signs for many words. Most educators suggest beginning with a small number of signs. This is because some believe more signs will confuse the baby.

You should begin with the number of signs that seems most comfortable for you. We offered you a starting point in chapter 5. There we suggested focusing on three very effective signs for early communication: EAT, MORE, and ALL DONE. This pattern has proven to be successful with many parents, and you may want to follow it.

However, other educators point out that parents do not typically restrict the number of spoken English words they use with their baby. Parents do not say, "Let's speak only three words because we do not want to confuse our child." Also, when people learn a second language they usually choose the total immersion method. So again, you get to make the final decision. Based on what you know, what you desire, and your own particular set of circumstances, what do you believe will work best for you and your baby?

Which Hand Should You Use?

Many signs require two hands, but many more are one-handed. For these one-handed signs, most people use their dominant hand as their primary signing hand. If they are left-handed, they use their left, and if they are right-handed, they use their right. But when it comes to signing with babies, often you won't have both hands free or your dominant hand will be busy. You'll sometimes have to be creative and modify signs. For example, LOVE can be signed with one hand across your chest, and ALL DONE has the same meaning if you use only one hand. (See examples on this page and next.)

Two-handed LOVE

One-handed LOVE

Two-handed ALL DONE   *One-handed ALL DONE*

You can also switch hands. If you are holding the baby in your dominant arm and can't use that hand, sign the word with your other hand. Again, the sign will have the same meaning.

EAT right-handed   *EAT left-handed*

Tips for Successful Signing

Here are some practical tips to use when signing with your baby. Keep them in mind and they will help you to be successful.

Have Your Baby's Attention

All babies are different and have individual characteristics. Early in your child's life, you will be able to gauge when your baby will be most responsive to you. It is a good idea to introduce the signs during times when you sense your baby is content and interested. Generally, some of the best times for this are meal time, bath time, or other special and playful times when you and your baby are interacting. When you notice your little one is looking at you, you can begin to sign. Speaking in an animated way with appropriate exaggerated facial expression will attract an infant's attention.

You can also touch your baby to gain attention. Some signs can be formed on the baby's body. WASH (see chapter 7) is an example of a sign that could be placed on the baby's arm to wash an arm, or on the cheek to wash a cheek, and so on. In this instance, you are doing tactile signing, another way to help your baby learn and remember words.

Place Signs Near Your Face

Your baby must be able to clearly see the sign. To achieve this, you should be on the same level as the baby. Traditionally signs are placed at about the midchest level. This works well for toddlers; however, with young babies it is best to place the sign nearer your face. Your face will offer a clue to the baby about the meaning of the sign. You should express the essence of the sign with your face as you form the sign with your hand. The baby should be able to easily see both your hand and your face.

Babies acquire a vast amount of knowledge between birth and their first birthday. This is a very short span of time in which to develop and learn an incredible amount of information, but using sign language actually gives babies a boost. When you offer this advantage to an infant, you will be more successful if you try to deliver all of the signs within the baby's sight lines.

Speak and Sign Together

Signing and speaking the words at the same time is important. Every time you say the word, sign the word. This gives your baby the sound of the word as well as the picture of the sign. By doing this, you are offering the word to the child through multiple senses. Your baby will come to understand what a word sounds, looks, and feels like. This is one of the key reasons signing is so effective. There is no better way to introduce language to a child.

Speak Clearly

Clearly enunciate the word you are saying and signing. Always use good standard English with your baby, and pronounce words clearly and distinctly. Do not use what is commonly called "baby talk." Do not expose your child to cartoons or media products created for infants and children that use poorly articulated words. Many cartoon characters do not speak clearly pronounced English. Be aware that children mimic the sounds of speech that they hear; that is why they often sound much like their parents. The best thing you can do to help little ones succeed in their future lives is to help them acquire a strong vocabulary and good speech.

Use Correct Signs

Always use the correct sign even though your baby may sign something different. In other words, try to consistently form each sign in the same, accurate manner. When your baby begins to sign to you, the signs will undoubtedly be immature, imperfect imitations. This is absolutely normal. As the infant continues to form signs, they will become clearer and more accurate. You can help your baby by never repeating an immature sign. Rather, repeat the sign correctly and say the word that was formed. This reinforces the signing behavior and provides an additional example of the sign for your baby to model.

Keep Signing Fun and Playful

Your signing activities should always be fun and playful. Never force your baby to sign. Look for fun and interesting ways to sign the words you are using in conversation or in other activities. Use exaggerated facial expressions to enhance the word and its meaning. This also helps to keep your baby's attention focused on you and the sign. Finally, praise and positively reward all efforts to communicate to you with sign.

How to Recognize Your Baby's Signs

When a baby begins to sign, the signs will not be perfect. They will be an approximation of the sign you have used. Your child will try to mimic or copy your sign, but just as children do not learn to speak perfect English with their first attempts, they will not use perfectly formed signs. It is critical for you to watch your baby closely so that you can recognize the first attempts at responding to your signs.

These first faltering attempts should be acknowledged and praised. Recognizing and praising early signing endeavors encourages your baby to continue to try to sign. Keep in mind that once your baby does begin to sign, you should continue to use the correct sign even if you recognize an approximation from your child. Just as with spoken language, the best way to teach signing is to speak clearly and sign correctly.

How can you improve or increase your ability to spot your infant's first signs? One way is to practice forming the signs in front of a mirror. This practice gives you a picture of the sign from the receiver's point of view. Of course, your baby's hand is much smaller than yours and differently shaped. However, doing this should significantly increase your chances of identifying your infant's first faltering attempts at signing. Acknowledging and praising these trials reinforces a baby's interest in communicating with signs.

When babies begin to sign, caregivers should learn to recognize the signs. Understanding and responding to babies' signs helps them continue to use signs. When the meaning of a baby's signs is consistently understood, responded to, and praised by all caregivers, the infant is encouraged to use more signs.

Signing Success Story

Susan thought she was well prepared to recognize her son's first signs. She was expecting to see EAT or ALL DONE since those were words she used consistently at meal times. She also used signs with books and had learned some animal signs and transportation signs.

Adam loved trains and had toy trains, books with trains, and blankets with trains because he seemed to like them so much. They even had to stop and watch anytime they encountered a train. She signed TRAIN to him whenever they talked about trains.

She noticed one day that he was rubbing his hands. She thought he had a sore or some other injury, but upon inspection all was okay. Susan kept watching for EAT or ALL DONE. Adam continued to rub his hands and then one day she realized that he was doing this right after she signed TRAIN. She was so surprised that she had not realized that the *rubbing was actually a sign: he was signing his version of TRAIN. Susan understood right then and there how she needed to watch for what her son was interested in or what he was trying to say, not what she thought he would do.*

TRAIN position one   TRAIN position two

TRAIN—Make the sign for the letter U with both hands, holding your palms down. Lay the fingers of your right hand on top of the fingers of your left. Then move the right-hand fingers back and forth on the left-hand fingers. Repeat.

Conclusion

You can begin signing with your baby at any time you like. Most nonsigners—people with no background in signing—generally begin when their baby is about 6 months old. Babies will begin to sign back sometime between 9 and 14 months old. Keeping a watchful eye for recognizable movements will help you respond to and reward your baby's attempts. We've provided the key points on successful signing in the appendix so that you can photocopy them and put them up in an easily accessible place (on the refrigerator, for example) for reference. This reminder will help you to remember to speak and sign words clearly, to sign a word every time you say it, to have your baby's attention, to use signs at meaningful times, to keep signing fun and playful, and to relate signs to objects or to specific needs or wants. You will find that all these tips become second nature very quickly. It is useful to provide grandparents and other caregivers with this information as well.

Chapter 7
Add More Signs

It's time to expand the number of signs you are using with your baby. So many parents have asked us, "What signs should I add next?" This chapter provides you with the signs we believe are most useful for communicating with babies. Parents all over the country use the signs included in this chapter successfully. These signs provide babies with words they can use to address their wants and needs. You can add them in the order offered here or choose your own direction. If you are a beginning signer, add just a few signs at a time until you are comfortable using them before moving on to additional signs. Whether you add all or only a few of these signs, you will ultimately be amazed at your child's ability to "speak" to you through sign language.

More Signs to Explore

Now that you've incorporated EAT, ALL DONE, and MORE into your life, we suggest adding these next three signs: MILK/BOTTLE, HURT, and SLEEP/BED. These signs help babies express important wants and needs in a way that others will comprehend. How wonderful it is for babies at 10, 12 or 14 months to be able to express themselves directly without having to resort to crying or screaming!

MILK / BOTTLE

MILK is a simple one-handed sign that is very easy for babies to do. Many parents, when signing with babies, use the sign for MILK for anything that comes out of a bottle; for instance, breast milk, formula, and water. MILK can also be used interchangeably for BOTTLE. Later, as your baby becomes more efficient at signing, or moves into the toddler years, you can use separate signs for MILK and BOTTLE.

MILK—Squeeze your hand repeatedly (as if you are milking a cow).

BOTTLE—Lay your left hand flat, palm up. Set your right hand on it as if you are holding a bottle, then lift it up, squeezing your hand together, representing how it narrows at the top.

HURT / OUCH

HURT or OUCH is a two-handed sign, like MORE. It is a directional sign, which means that when you sign the word HURT, you sign it near where you hurt (or where your child is hurting). For example, if you bumped your knee you would say, "I HURT my knee," and sign the word HURT near your knee; if you bumped your head, you would sign HURT near your head. You

can ask and sign near your ear, "Does your ear HURT?" You can create signing opportunities, for example, on yourself and say "OUCH, I HURT my head."

HURT / OUCH—With both hands in fists, point index fingers toward each other and tap the fingertips together. Remember that this sign is directional. Sign it near the place where you hurt.

Signing Success Story

For Ken and Georgia, HURT has proven over and over to be an important sign to use. When their daughter Coreen was about 12 months old, she woke up a little fussy after a nap one day and began to sign the word HURT near her ear. They knew she had an ear infection, something she seemed to get regularly. They immediately arranged to take her to the doctor.

When the doctor looked into Coreen's ear, he said, "How did you know to bring her in? The ear infection is very early on."

They answered, "She told us."

"Told you?"

"Yes!" They explained how they had been using sign language with her and that she signed to them that her ear hurt.

"Well, you may have guessed correctly, but I'm not sure she can actually tell you these things," the doctor said.

Now 20 years later, their 14-month-old grandson Richie woke up and signed to his mom that his ear hurt. So Sarah, just like Ken and Georgia had done years before with Coreen, took him to the doctor. She explained that Richie had signed to her that his ear hurt. Sure enough, he had the beginnings of an ear infection. But this time the doctor's response was different.

"I'm hearing a lot of good things about signing with babies for early communication," he said.

SLEEP / BED

Babies begin to get very fussy when they are tired and need to go to sleep. The sign for SLEEP and BED is the same. So whether or not you say bed or sleep, you will sign the same word. "Do you want to go to SLEEP?" or "It's time to go to BED." This sign is often used in combination with the word tired. "Are you SLEEPY, are you TIRED?" Many parents use the sign SLEEP interchangeably for TIRED at first and then, like MILK and BOTTLE, you can use separate signs for each word.

SLEEP / BED—With your head bent, close your eyes and rest your cheek on the palm of your flat hand (as if you are pretending to be asleep). You may also encounter this as a two handed sign, with both hands held together and under a cheek. Either version is fine.

TIRED—Hold your hands flat, bent at the knuckles, with the palms facing in, fingertips touching at your shoulders. Roll your hands downward on your fingertips. Use with a tired facial expression and posture.

Continue Adding Signs

The following signs in this chapter can be introduced at this stage. Pick and choose the signs that fit best into your life and your needs.

CHANGE / DIAPER

As parents, you have all kinds of clues when your baby needs a diaper change—the aroma, the sound, and even your child's actions and cries. With ASL you can now add a word or two that provide a way for babies to tell parents they need a diaper change without crying. Many parents have found CHANGE to be easier for their baby to sign than DIAPER. Some have told us that if they signed the two words together, even if their baby signed only CHANGE at first, eventually, the baby added DIAPER to the signing vocabulary.

CHANGE—Make the letter X with both hands, one on top of the other, with your palms facing each other. Twist your hands so that they switch position. The opposite hand is now on top.

DIAPER—Hold your index and middle fingers out and together with your thumb pointing down, near your waist, and open and close your fingers (as if you are opening and closing a pin on a diaper).

Use CHANGE every time you change or are about to change your baby's diaper, and say, "Do you need a diaper CHANGE?" or "I think it's time to CHANGE your diaper." You can also sign both words when you say, "Okay, let's CHANGE your DIAPER."

HELP

HELP is a good interactive sign. When a baby is frustrated with something—trying to reach a toy, for example, or trying to take off a shoe—it's a good opportunity to use this sign and connect it to the action saying, "Would you like Mommy to HELP you?" or "Let Daddy HELP you with that" or "Mommy will HELP you to pick up the toys" or "Do you want me to HELP you to put something away?" You can use HELP along with almost anything you are doing. This is a two-handed sign, but you can also sign it one-handed, especially since moms often have one of their two hands full.

HELP—Hold one hand in a fist, thumb up, and the other hand flat, palm up. Lay your fist on top of your palm. Then lift both hands (as if one hand is helping the other). Use only your fist hand whenever you cannot make a two-handed sign.

DRINK

As your baby moves from a bottle to a cup, the sign for DRINK can help you distinguish between drinking from a bottle and drinking from a cup. DRINK is a very iconic sign; that is, the sign looks like the action of taking a drink from a cup. As you learn signing, you will find many more signs like this.

When introducing signs, it is a good idea to have something to which you can connect each sign. In this case, DRINK can be connected to a cup. So when you ask, "Do you want a DRINK?" be sure to show the cup or bottle and, after you sign the word, offer it to your baby to drink. Try to create signing opportunities for you to use and demonstrate this word. For example, "Mommy wants a DRINK" or "Mommy's going to DRINK some water now."

DRINK—Shape your hand as if you are holding a glass, then bring it up to your mouth and tip it towards you so that it looks as if you're drinking from that glass.

BATH

One of the fun times in a baby's daily life is bath time. All babies seem to enjoy splashing around in warm water with toys and spending playful time with Mom or Dad. BATH is one of the first signs to use because babies usually look forward to this time and you have their attention.

BATH—Hold your fists, thumbs up, at the sides of your chest, then rub up and down repeatedly (as if you are washing your chest).

WASH

When babies begin to crawl, their mobility opens up a whole new world to explore, learn about, and experience. Along with this comes dirty hands, knees, faces, and more. WASH is a fun and easy sign to learn and can very easily be used in conjunction with BATH. WASH is an iconic sign, like DRINK; when you form it, you look like you are washing your hands.

WASH is also a directional sign, like HURT, meaning that to WASH your baby's face, you have to make the sign near the cheek, or to WASH your baby's knee, you have to make it at the knee. You can always demonstrate on yourself, saying, "Mommy has to WASH her arm" or nose, and so on.

WASH—Make fists with both hands, right palm down and left palm up. Rub the right hand in a circular motion over the left hand. Repeat.

This can be a fun sign to use at bath time. You can incorporate it into an old nursery rhyme by singing "This is the way we wash our hands." You can adapt this rhyme to "This is the way we WASH your hands," and sign WASH on your baby's hands, then expand on this to wash other body parts; for example, "This is the way we WASH your head" or tummy, and so on.

HOT and COLD

HOT and COLD are helpful signs that can be used for everything including food, bath time, clothing, and bedtime. A bottle can be too HOT, or the water in the bath can be too COLD. Wearing a jacket can be too HOT or a baby may be COLD and needs another blanket. You can use these signs around the house. HOT can be a safety warning sign when your child becomes mobile. The stove is HOT. The coffee cup is HOT. The light bulb is HOT. COLD can be demonstrated in a playful way: ice cream is COLD, the refrigerator is COLD, and so on.

HOT—Hold your curved hand, fingers spread, near your mouth, palm in. Then, in a quick motion, pull your hand away, turning it outward and down a little (as if you're getting rid of something hot very fast).

COLD—Make the letter S with both hands and hold them at chest level, palms facing each other. Shake them from side to side with hunched shoulders (as if you are cold).

Be creative in incorporating these signs into your baby's life, saying, "Is the water too HOT?" "Is your bottle too COLD?" "Mommy's COLD" or "Daddy's food is too HOT."

GENTLE

This is a sign that works well to help your baby understand how to play with siblings, other children, and pets. It is useful to say and sign the word and then demonstrate the meaning of GENTLE. For example, say and sign GENTLE and then pet an animal, saying, "GENTLE, be GENTLE, and pet the kitty."

GENTLE—Hold one hand flat, palm down. Then gently stroke the back of that hand.

I LOVE YOU

I LOVE YOU is such a wonderful phrase for parents to say to their babies. This warm and affectionate phrase not only provides comfort and security, but it bonds mother, father, and baby together. I LOVE YOU makes us, even as adults, feel good. Babies thrive in an environment of love, affection, safety, security, and parental interaction. I LOVE YOU strongly supports everything we try to do for our babies.

You can sign I LOVE YOU in two ways. One way uses a quick and simple single-handed sign. Georgia and Ken used this sign with their children. As their children grew into teenagers, Georgia and Ken could sign I LOVE YOU from a distance, without calling it out and embarrassing their teenage sensitivity.

I LOVE YOU (shorthand, slang version)—Hold your hand up near your shoulder, palm out, with your ring and middle fingers down, your index and little fingers up, and your thumb out. Keep this sign stationary; if you move it around, you could be signing JET. Sometimes movement changes the meaning of a sign.

You can also use three separate signs for the words I, LOVE, and YOU. LOVE is a fun sign because it looks and feels like a great, big hug. It looks a little bit like how LOVE should be. Here are the signs for each word in case you want to use them with your baby.

I / ME—Hold a fist up with your index finger out, and point it to the middle of your chest.

LOVE—Make fists, crossed at the wrist, and hold them against your chest (as if you are holding something you love).

YOU—Make a fist hand, and point your index finger out and toward the person to whom you are talking.

Signs for Feelings

The signs that represent the basic emotions all human beings experience are another category of words that are helpful for a baby to learn and begin to comprehend. The emotions happy, sad, and mad often engender actions such as crying or smiling. Learning the ASL signs for these words and actions can help you communicate emotions to your baby.

HAPPY and SMILE

HAPPY is a sign babies can learn when they are quite young. It is a sign that expresses a good feeling. Using this sign can encourage an infant to SMILE more and attempt to mimic the happy face you offer as you make the sign and say the word.

HAPPY—Hold your hands flat, palms in and thumbs up. Brush your chest in a circular motion. Use with a happy facial expression. Repeat.

SMILE—Hold flat hands slightly bent, with your fingertips near the sides of your mouth. Then move your hands up each side of your cheeks (as if you are drawing a smile).

SAD and CRY

Another feeling sign is SAD. Because of what the word connotes, this may not be a favorite sign to teach your child. However, babies do feel sad and out of sorts sometimes, and it is helpful to identify this emotion and label it. SAD usually comes with crying.

SAD—Hold your hands flat, fingers spread and palms facing in, at eye level and then move them down a little. Use with a sad facial expression.

CRY—Bring both extended index fingers up to your face, palms facing in, and then move them down your cheeks, alternating sides, as if tears are rolling down your cheeks.

MAD / ANGRY

A baby feels mad or angry at an early age. When you know your child is mad, this sign offers you a way to get the child's attention, make eye contact, and begin the process of calming the child down.

MAD / ANGRY—Hold your hands up with the fingertips curved, palms in front of your chin. Then squeeze your fingers together just a little and move hand slightly toward your chin. Use an angry facial expression.

Name Signs

Name signs have been used for many years. They are the signs people use to signify each other. Typically people do not make up their own name signs; the signs are given to them by others.

For example, when Deaf children were educated in residential schools, their school would often bestow a name sign on them. Sometimes the name sign included a sign or manual letter that stood for the school. Many name signs are the first initial of a person's name signed at the shoulder, or the initial combined with a word sign that illustrates a specific characteristic. For instance, Marilyn's name sign, given to her by a Deaf ASL teacher, is the manual letter M sweeping across the palm in the sign for NICE. Georgia was given the name sign of GIRL at the School for the Deaf where she worked because she was the only "girl" counselor.

Following this example, you can give the people in your family or other persons important in your child's life name signs to indicate or signify them when you are referring to them. Try to maintain the historical pattern for establishing these name signs. For Mommy and Daddy, use the signs for MOTHER and FATHER.

FATHER / DADDY—Tap the thumb of your flat hand, fingers spread and pointing up, on your forehead. Repeat.

MOTHER / MOMMY—Tap the thumb of your flat hand, fingers spread, on your chin. Repeat.

You can use the sign for BABY to indicate your baby. Depending on the infant's name and those who would use the sign, you may want to confer a name sign on the child. This is a lovely opportunity to involve the entire family in observing their newest member and creating a name sign that will express one of the baby's discernible attributes.

The manual letter S is often used for sister and the manual letter B for brother. The ASL signs for brother and sister are fairly complicated for a small baby to form. Sometimes the manual letter is combined with a sign like NICE, but many times it stands alone to represent the sibling. It is often the first letter of the child's name.

For pets, you can either use the animal signs—DOG, CAT, BIRD, FISH, and so on or give them name signs. When you give name signs to your pets, you enable your baby to identify the pets and actually "call" them well before your child acquires any verbal speech.

These name signs can aid your child's comprehension and will allow an infant to more fully be part of the family. In most instances, your baby will quite quickly be able to understand to whom you are referring when you indicate the person with a name sign as well as a spoken word.

Growing Your Signs

As you and your baby grow with signing, you will find that you want to add other signs. Part 3 of this book offers a variety of signing activities that you can begin to do with your baby. These activities will not only help you expand your signing vocabulary, but they also will provide interactive fun for you and your baby all the way through childhood. We believe that babies, toddlers, preschoolers, and beyond will benefit from interactive signing activities.

A reminder may be in order at this point: you do not need to learn and teach your child every sign in this book. Select the ones that fit your and your baby's lives. For example, your child may love trains and want to sign TRAIN often but show very little interest in signing BIRD. If this happens, focus on what your child enjoys and keep offering other signs you think will be of interest. For example, if you know you are going to the zoo, learn a few of the signs for the animals you may be seeing; or if you're going to the park, learn some signs you can use there. If you live in an apartment house, you may want to teach your child the sign for ELEVATOR; if you live on a farm, you might want to teach your child the sign for COW. If you have a dog in your home, you may want to use the sign for DOG. If your child enjoys jumping in a Jolly Jumper or similar device, try signing JUMP the way Noah's parents did in the upcoming story.

BIRD—Hold your right hand by your mouth, with your index finger and thumb pointed out. Open and close these fingers, imitating the movement of a bird's beak.

DOG / PUPPY—With a flat hand, tap the side of your hip. Then bring your hand up and snap your fingers.

COW—Make the sign for Y with your hand. Hold your thumb on the side of your head and rotate your little finger forward with a twist of your hand (representing the horn on a cow).

ELEVATOR—Hold up your flat left hand with the palm facing right. Then make an E (see glossary) with your right hand, and move it up and down on your left hand so it looks like an elevator.

Signing Success Story

Danica began signing with Noah when he was 4 months old. She used the typical signs, such as MILK, MORE, and EAT, but she also included the signs for activities Noah particularly enjoyed. When he was about 5 months old, he started using a Jolly Jumper. Because Noah liked his Jolly Jumper so much, Danica and Noah's dad began to use the sign for JUMP before they would put him in his jumper. They would preface the action with an enthusiastic JUMP sign and a question like "Do you want to JUMP in your Jolly Jumper, Noah?"

One day when Noah was about 6 months old, he was jumping in his Jolly Jumper while Danica was on the telephone. He stopped jumping and looked at his mom. He seemed to have had enough jumping. She was in the middle of her conversation, so she raised her hand to her other open hand and enthusiastically signed "JUMP, JUMP," with a big smile of encouragement on her face. Right after that, Noah resumed jumping in his Jolly Jumper with a big smile on his face!

During the following week, Noah started to use the JUMP sign himself. Whenever he did, his mom or dad would put him in his Jolly Jumper and he would jump to his heart's content.

This account is a fine example of a mom using signs for activities her baby enjoys. Doing this gives a child a stronger reason to attempt to form a sign and use it to communicate and to engage in an activity again. The sign for JUMP is a particularly good one because it is iconic—it looks just like someone jumping. It is also a sign that is easy for a baby to replicate with enough accuracy for a parent to comprehend.

JUMP—Hold one hand flat with your palm up. Extend the index and middle fingers of the other hand out to represent legs, and place them on the flat hand. Then make the motion of jumping up from your flat hand.

Conclusion

In all your signing activities, whether taking a walk, playing around the house, using rhymes, singing songs, or reading stories, you get to choose how much or how little you want to incorporate signing into your lives. We are offering suggestions based on experience, but signing with your baby is personal to you and your child. Keep the signing fun, and together you will not only increase communication but have years of quality interactive experiences.

PART 3

Signing in Your Everyday Life and Activities

Chapter 8
Make Signing a Habit

Try to make signing a habit. Even though we have suggested you gain your baby's attention first, this will not always be possible. Sometimes when your child is clearly focused on you, a noise may occur or another person may enter the room. Your child will be attracted to the new stimulus and cease paying attention to you. When this happens, do not be stressed. Continue to sign and speak. If you are consistent, patient, and calm, your baby will soon be signing back to you. We do not know of any baby that didn't eventually begin to sign if the parents stuck with it. So do make it a habit.

Tips for Signing Every Day

Many of your interactions with your child will revolve around activities that are repeated several times each day. Focus on these daily activities as a natural starting point. The signs that represent eating, resting, and bathing are particularly suited to be the first ASL vocabulary that you introduce to your baby.

You have many choices of signs to use, and there are no hard and fast rules. For instance, most babies begin life drinking milk. Your baby will either be breast-fed, be drinking milk or formula from a bottle, or perhaps a combination of the two. As we discussed earlier, you can use the sign for MILK when talking about a bottle. You can also use MILK to represent breast-feeding, or you may decide the sign for BOTTLE is more appropriate. These choices are yours to make.

Bathing is a daily routine virtually all parents will represent with the same sign—BATH. So you are relieved of decision making. As was previously explained, babies usually love to make this sign, particularly if they enjoy their baths. But this brings up an important point. If your baby does not enjoy bathing, skip this sign because the baby will have little desire to learn it. When you integrate signs in your baby's daily routine, strive to focus on signs for activities that are pleasurable.

Diaper changing is another time where you can gain your baby's attention and sign words that will enable communication. As we discussed, you can use the sign CHANGE to communicate the need to CHANGE a diaper, or you can decide to use the word DIAPER. You can add other words like MORE and ALL DONE: "Would you like MORE powder (or lotion)?" "Do you want to play MORE before I put your DIAPER on?" You can even say, "We're ALL DONE CHANGING your DIAPER." This kind of creative use of words at a time when your baby is focused on you will help you teach signs and reinforce your baby's learning.

Do It Your Way

Most parents would agree that each baby is a unique individual. Some scholars believe that an infant's unique and innate cerebral characteristics are often ignored. Disregarding the individual nature of an infant's mind is a serious blunder, according to Howard Gardner, the originator of the Multiple Intelligences theory (see pages 16 and 17). Gardner points out in *Intelligence*

Reframed that uniform education, or training every child in the same manner, is antagonistic to his theory of multiple intelligences.[1]

The suggestions you find in this book are based on research, anecdotal reports, and the personal experiences of the authors. They represent techniques that have proven to be successful with infants. But these are only suggestions that you can adapt to your own baby, yourself, and your family. Incorporate your own ideas in this blueprint. Find specific words that fit the activities your infant enjoys. Select the signs that are comfortable for you to use with your baby as you both learn to communicate with each other.

Signing Activities

Spending quality time with your child is one of the best ways to enhance early learning, create strong parent-child bonds, and generate an enthusiasm for learning that will last a lifetime. Studies have shown repeatedly that a key factor in educational success is the time spent by parents in the early years by talking, signing, reading, playing, singing, and, in general, being involved with their young children.

Parents must be responsive to the behavioral cues that babies give. A baby's attention span is relatively short, so being able to move from one playtime activity to another with ease helps parents to keep babies engaged and interested. When your child wants to stop an activity, stop. If your child wants to repeat it, do it again. If your child wants to move on to another activity, follow along. Let your child help direct where the activities lead.

Signing adds another level of fun and physical involvement to activities. Increasing the number of signs you know will assist you in moving from one activity to another and still include signs. You will find the word SIGN to be helpful in getting your baby to learn and recall words.

SIGN—Make fists with both hands, extend the index fingers, and hold them pointing up. Then move your hands in large, alternating circles toward the chest.

Signing on a Walk

Often you will take walks with your baby in a carriage or stroller. As soon as the infant is able to see from the carriage or stroller, you can begin to point out interesting sights as they come into view. A colorful BIRD or a big HOUSE or perhaps a beautiful TREE or FLOWER may attract your child as you stroll your neighborhood. It is a good idea to name and sign at least three or four things you encounter on your walk.

BIRD—Hold your right hand by your mouth, with your index finger and thumb pointed out. Open and close these fingers, imitating the movement of a bird's beak.

HOUSE—With the fingertips of your hands touching, move your flat hands from the center of the "roof" out to the "walls" and then down (as if you are drawing the outline of the roof and walls of a house).

TREE—Hold your left arm across your body, palm down. Place the elbow of your right arm on top of your left hand, with your right hand flat, pointing up with loose fingers and facing left. Twist your right hand back and forth. This sign looks like a tree. Repeat.

FLOWER—Hold the fingertips of one hand together (as in the sign for EAT) and touch each side of your nose (as if you are smelling a flower).

The three or four items you select to identify for your child should be repeated and pointed out each time you take the same walk. Your baby may not sign each of these signs back to you but will begin to understand that all things have names, and your baby will show a heightened interest in them.

If your child seems to pay particular attention to something seen on the walk, name this item and then show the sign for it. If you do not know the sign, look it up when you get home so you can connect the sign and word for the object each time you encounter it on your walks. If you have a picture of the object, you can show it and then say and sign the word. Be patient, and your child will soon be repeating the sign for you.

Activities like this increase your child's understanding of the general concept that objects have names. Try to select objects you routinely use, and always include any object in which your baby has shown some interest. For more signs to increase you and your baby's vocabularies, see chapter 9 for songs and rhymes, or go to the Glossary of Signs and choose signs that are of interest to your baby.

Signing with an Object

Up to this point, most of the signs have represented a feeling the baby appears to be experiencing or a daily activity in which you routinely engage, such as eating. You may even have labeled the people and pets in your child's world with name signs. Additionally, perhaps you have identified a few objects and now sign them as you regularly pass them on walks around your neighborhood.

Another effective approach to engaging your baby in signing is to sign the names of various objects as you point to them. For example, when you feed your child with a spoon, you can hold the spoon and make the sign for SPOON. You can play a hide-and-seek game with the object and introduce the concept of WHERE. Ask, "WHERE is your CUP?" as you sign and say CUP. Then say, "Look, this is your CUP" as you show the cup in one hand and sign in the other. Next, say, "WHERE is your SPOON?" Then, "Look, this is the SPOON" while you produce the spoon, holding it in one hand as you make the sign with the other. Many objects can be identified this way, such as BALL, BANANA, and COOKIE. Set common objects in front of the baby and say and sign what they are. Then move from one to another and back to maintain your baby's interest.

WHERE—Hold your index finger up and wave it from side to side.

CUP—Hold your left hand flat. Shape your right hand as if you are holding a cup, and then lift it. Repeat.

SPOON—Hold your left hand flat, palm up and slightly cupped. With your right hand make the letter U (see glossary) and make a scooping motion down, across, and up from the left hand. It will look as if you are using a spoon. Repeat.

BALL—*With your fingers spread and curved, tap the fingertips of both hands together at chest level. Repeat.*

BANANA—*Hold one index finger up, palm forward; then with the other hand, pretend you are peeling a banana from the top of your raised index finger down. The first motion is near the back of the index finger and the second motion is near the front.*

COOKIE—*Hold your left hand flat, palm up. Curve the fingers of your right hand to form a circle (as if touching all sides of a round cookie). Then touch your left palm twice, once directly on it and the second twisted slightly so it looks as if you are using a cookie cutter.*

Naming and signing objects for a baby has several more benefits. This activity stimulates eye gaze. It can become an active communication interaction between you and your baby, like a game. Finally, babies are actually learning the name of a variety of objects. Because they are looking at and often making the sign for an object, they have a much better chance of remembering its name. This playful interaction can be a great help to your baby's language development.

Signing with a Storybook

Introducing a baby to books and stories is a pleasure most parents anticipate. There is joy in sharing this quiet time with your child as you recall similar experiences you had during your own childhood days. Those of us who love words cannot think of a better activity to do with our babies than read to them and share our enthusiasm for literature.

Other parents, not quite as fond of these activities, have surely heard that reading to a child is a significant step that is needed for the child's strong academic development. For such parents, adding signs can often make the reading process more appealing. There is more action and physical involvement with reading when even a little bit of signing is included.

When you sit down to read a book with your baby, you will usually introduce one sign to represent a main idea from the book. For instance, a much loved and often read early childhood book is *Goodnight Moon*. The sign most moms and dads use with this book is MOON. The moon is basically the main character in the book, and the word itself is often repeated. The moon is also an object in the night sky that can regularly be pointed out to a child. Partially due to its initial M sound, MOON is a word that many babies can pronounce easily and early. By teaching your baby the sign and pronouncing the word clearly and distinctly when you sign it as you are reading the story, or by pointing out the moon in the night sky, you will be helping to encourage earlier speech for your baby.

As you choose books for you and your baby to read, you can find signs for some of the words in the signing glossary. Learn the sign for BUNNY when reading and signing *The Runaway Bunny* or the sign for CATERPILLAR for *The Very Hungry Caterpillar*. Picture books allow you to choose a variety of signs to use with your baby. Point to an image on a page, then say and sign the

word for that image. Be sure to have your baby's attention—first to the image and then to the sign.

BOOK—Hold your flat hands together at chest level. Open your hands while keeping the little fingers touching (as if you are opening a book).

READ—Hold your left hand up, your palm facing to the right. With the other hand, make the letter V, point the fingertips toward your left hand, and then move them from side to side and down (as if the right hand is reading words in a book).

MOON—Hold a fist with your thumb and index finger out and curved (as if you are making the letter C), then tap the side of your head with your thumb. This looks like a crescent moon. Repeat.

RABBIT/BUNNY—Cross both hands at the wrist with your index and middle fingers and thumb extended. Bend your fingers up and down with a double motion (like the ears on a bunny).

CATERPILLAR—Hold one arm out horizontally, and hold the other hand in a fist with your index finger out. Wiggle your index finger as you move your hand up your arm so it looks like a caterpillar crawling along.

Signing and Television

Television is a part of almost every American baby's home life. It is a reality that can't be ignored, and it can be used well. Television is a modern technological mobile. Parents today often use it to entertain their babies in the same way parents of past generations used mobiles hanging over a crib or playpen. Just like mobiles, television can offer interesting stimulation and entertainment. Responsible television can also provide wonderful images, interesting sounds, and music. Often this medium offers experiences that babies would not have without television viewing and listening.

Five things are important when choosing television programming for your baby.

1. Consider whether or not the program is age appropriate for your baby.
2. Watch the program with your baby and observe whether or not the child maintains interest.
3. Keep in mind that babies enjoy activities for short periods of time so programming that reflects this is preferred.
4. Interact with your baby's television viewing. Engage the child and point out objects, or laugh when something silly happens.
5. Repetition is key to learning and it is common for babies to enjoy the same thing over and over.

Quality signing DVD products and programs can be used to actively involve your baby with images, music, and signs while reinforcing the vocabulary that you are trying to build. Watching television is also a good way for you and your baby to learn signs together. These signs can then be worked into your daily life and into other fun activities. Choose quality programming, be actively involved, and use the lessons learned at other times during the day to enhance your use of television.

Signing Success Story

Joan's daughter Jennifer loves to watch children's music DVDs. She loves the music and songs and especially enjoys songs with movements and signing.

Jennifer and Joan learned lots of signs from singing and signing along with the We Sign Play Time DVD. Later as they played, they would sing and sign the songs or parts of the songs they had been watching. They learned so many signs, and the songs made it easy to remember them. Joan wasn't sure how many Jennifer was remembering until one summer afternoon in their pool.

Jennifer, who was then about 14 months old, tried over and over to say a word but Joan could not understand it. She also saw that Jennifer was using one of her hands up by her mouth. It looked like she was signing, but again, what was she saying? Joan just didn't get it at first. Then she heard a familiar sound, a mockingbird, and realized that what Jennifer was signing was BIRD. She had learned to sign the word from singing one of the songs on the DVD and when she heard the mockingbird she was clearly signing BIRD.

It would be months before Jennifer would say the word bird, but she signed it whenever she saw or heard one. She clearly learned and understood this word and later would learn and use many other words by watching television and participating in the signing songs on the DVD.

BIRD—Hold your right hand by your mouth, with your index finger and thumb pointed out. Open and close these fingers, imitating the movement of a bird's beak.

Your Signing Journal

A wonderful way to be involved in your baby's signing is to keep a signing journal. You can incorporate this information into almost any of the "baby record" books available. You can also create your own journal by using blank art books that are available at stationery and art supply stores. It's fun to add pictures and decorations to make each page special. You can access sample journal pages on-line at http://www.signtospeak.com. Use the code STSB109A to download the forms.

Keeping a journal of your ongoing signing endeavors will provide you with a rewarding experience. A written record helps you know when you introduced a particular sign and when the baby first used the sign or an approximation of it. It also helps you to remember all the signs that your baby has used so you can continue to use them and add new words. Furthermore, this written record will provide you with wonderful memories. Your journal will record fun moments, special signing events, favorite signing activities, and much more.

We have put together a list of topics that you can write about in your journal. Don't feel limited to these topics. Write about any and all things that interest you. Here are some suggestions to consider:

❀ Your child's name

❀ Your child's age when you began signing

❀ The first signs you used with your child

❀ The first word your child signed to you

❀ Your child's age when this happened

❀ The story about how and when your child used this first sign

❁ Your feelings about your child's first signing experience

❀ Reasons you wanted to sign with your child

❀ The second word your child signed to you

❀ Your child's age when this happened

❁ The story about how and when your child used this second sign

❀ Other favorite signs your child used

❀ Your special signing times with your child

❀ Other favorite signs your child has learned to sign

❁ Stories about how and when your child began to sign these words

❀ Your favorite signs and reasons you liked them

❀ Mom's favorite signing memory

❀ Dad's favorite signing memory

❁ Other special signing moments with your child

❀ Your child's favorite song to sign

❀ Your child's favorite rhyme to sign

❀ Your child's favorite book to sign

❁ Your child's favorite word to sign

❀ Signing activities your child especially liked

❀ Your reflections on signing with your child as a *baby*

These topics will help you get started keeping a written record of your baby's signing activities. As you come up with your own ideas, you will find that you will have many signing stories to write about. Reading journals is a fun way to look back on experiences that you and your baby had, along with enjoyable memories that you can share for years to come.

For journal page downloads, see our Sign to Speak On-line section at the end of the book.

Caregivers, Grandparents, and Siblings

It is best if all of the baby's caregivers use signs with the baby. However, sometimes this is not feasible. Some caregivers may feel uncomfortable using signs. Frequently, the mom is very enthusiastic about signing and finds it very easy to use signs as she communicates with her infant. If other caregivers such as the dad, grandparents, or siblings are troubled with signing, it is undoubtedly best that the mom proceed on her own. After your baby starts to sign, the other caregivers who were initially reluctant to try may be impressed by signing, think it looks like fun, and decide they want to sign with your baby as well.

Helpers

A good time to involve others is when you first begin to learn some signs, perhaps before your baby has arrived. Grandparents, the dad, family members, and other caregivers can learn the signs along with you. Ask them to help you master the signs and practice them with you. You can start with the simple Jump Start on Smart signs in chapter 5. We have also provided you with 12 Everyday Signs in the Babies Can Talk Toolbox for you to copy and give to everyone to help them with their signing.

Getting everyone involved will serve several purposes. Not only will it get more people signing with your baby, but it will help you learn how to form the signs and provide good practice as you instruct them. When others make the signs for you, you will get experience in recognizing the signs from the perspective of a receiver. As helpers make the signs, you should say the word and also make the sign.

This is great practice all around. Both young and old helpers will be creating new synapses in their brains while learning ASL vocabulary. Older helpers, such as grandparents, may be able to alleviate some of the distress of arthritis by using their hands and fingers to form the signs. And everyone will be increasing their familiarity with the signs the baby will learn and produce.

Siblings

If your baby has older siblings, you can use them to help you teach the new infant how to sign and communicate. This is an exciting and important activity for brothers and sisters. They will feel needed and useful as they introduce the ASL signs for English words to the newest family member.

Try to recall the first words your older child or children spoke. You can select the same words for the baby and use the ASL signs with the spoken

English. If the older children know that these were their first spoken words, they will undoubtedly be very enthusiastic about teaching the same words along with the signs to their new sister or brother.

Often slightly older children are unable to help care for the new babies. They cannot feed, change, or carry them. However, if they know some ASL signs, they can teach the new little one. This is a helpful activity they can engage in with some degree of competence. Sometimes older children will touch and shape the baby's hand into the proper sign, and move it to the correct location. As long as they do this gently, it should encourage the baby to move independently. Toddlers usually enjoy the opportunity to help care for the baby and anticipate the prospect of communicating more fully with the infant.

Signing Success Story

Alana had taught her son Cody some ASL signs when he was about a year old. Cody loved to sign, and as he began to talk, he would often speak and sign words simultaneously. Based on Cody's apparent pleasure and success with signing, Alana decided to begin to sign earlier with his baby sister, Jordan. Jordan was signed to from about 2 months of age.

Cody was quite an influence on his baby sister. He would almost always sign while speaking words to her. Cody also signed new words he understood but was unable to articulate. He tended to sign directly to his little sister by following the example of his mother.

One day when Alana was feeding Jordan her lunch, Alana signed and said EAT each time she offered Jordan a spoonful of green beans. Jordan folded the fingers of her right hand together and *brought them up to her ear and smiled. She kept doing it each time her mother signed EAT.*

Although this was not the perfect hand-to-mouth sign, Jordan had apparently understood and had started to form an immature sign. As Alana continued to feed her, this time peaches, Jordan continued to make the same sign.

Cody came into the kitchen and was very excited to see that his baby sister could sign. Jordan was a mere 6 1/2 months old, and she was signing. Jordan continued to sign EAT in this manner for a week or so, and then she gradually adjusted her sign and began to place her hand nearer her mouth. Undoubtedly, Cody helped facilitate this change because he consistently signed EAT correctly for her.

Conclusion

The more members of your family that sign with your baby, the better. Use the 12 Everyday Signs page in the Babies Can Talk Toolbox as a quick reference of baby signs. Photocopy the page and give it to the grandparents, aunts, uncles, and all other caregivers. Encourage them to sign with your baby. Once your baby is signing back, the list can help these family members be more aware of the signs.

Signing can greatly improve your child's vocabulary, and by including it in daily activities, such as reading books and singing songs, or taking walks, you will be enlarging your baby's usable vocabulary. Keeping a signing journal will help you to remember all the signs you've used and provide a record of when and how you introduced them, which you can use with later children. In the next chapter you will expand the activities that enhance your baby's signing vocabulary by signing with songs and rhymes.

Chapter 9
Use Signing with Songs and Rhymes

Parents often use the same songs and rhymes they learned as young children with their own babies. Traditional Mother Goose and nursery rhymes are timeless favorites. These are the tunes parents know well and enjoy sharing with their baby.

No matter what songs, rhymes, or chants you decide to use with your baby, keep it simple. Don't try to sign every word. Pick out a few of the signs for key words and use them over and over. Ken and Georgia had three goals in mind when choosing a song to sign with their babies. First, they looked for songs that were fun and age-appropriate—for babies, that means simple, short, and repetitive. Second, they chose songs that allowed them to reinforce the learning of specific signs they were working on, such as EAT or MORE. Third, they tried to offer songs and rhymes that had connections to early learning and vocabulary growth. For example, they looked for rhymes that allowed them to use animal signs, object signs, food signs, or feeling signs. In this way, they acquired lots of signs to use as their children grew.

Signing and Singing

Singing, as part of human life, predates writing. It is part of our humanity, and we have always recognized its importance. All people, everywhere in the world, create music. People have used music to pass on traditions and culture, to teach lessons, to tell history, to bond socially, and to entertain for thousands of years.

Music has been demonstrated to have many positive effects on babies and children, and music combined with movement has proven to be a powerful memory and recall activity. Think about movement songs like the "Itsy Bitsy Spider" or "Wheels on the Bus." We learned them as children and still firmly recall them as adults.

By combining music and songs with the movement and visual nature of sign language, you are providing babies and children with a wonderfully rich learning experience. Signing with songs encourages musical, verbal, visual, physical, and interactive learning all at the same time. Over 2,000 years ago, Confucius understood the power of involving someone in a learning experience. He said, "If you tell me, I will forget. If you show me, I may remember. If you involve me, I will understand."

For centuries, parents have used rhymes and songs to play with their babies. By enhancing these age-old activities with signing, parents can now provide babies with meaningful early learning. Fergus P. Hughes wrote in his book *Children, Play, and Development,* "Creative movement stimulates children to encode information about the world physically, or motorically, as well as intellectually, and to realize that there are many ways of knowing."[1] In other words, the movement and visual nature of signing, added creatively to songs and other interesting activities, provides a way for babies to learn and remember things in many different ways, using a wide variety of the learning styles.

Tips for Signing with Songs and Rhymes

Singing songs and rhymes with babies is easy and, as with signing skills, you don't need to be a great singer or have any singing experience. Babies enjoy the interaction, the language, rhyme, melody, and the comfort of their parent's voice. So you can learn a few signs for songs that you know, and then sing and sign or even speak and sign them to your baby. Here are some tips to keep in mind.

- **Have your baby's attention.** Be sure that the child is focused on you and what you are doing. If your baby drifts, try to regain the child's attention.

- **Follow your baby's cues.** If the child's attention turns to something new, sing and include signs for the new area of interest.

- **Keep the activity simple.** Sign just a few words, especially for babies, unless you are very familiar with sign language. Reuse these words over and over in various ways.

- **Keep the activity fun and playful.** Always have fun with your baby when playing. Never coerce or force your baby to engage in an activity. At this age, the connection with you is very important. The songs and signs or the books and other activities can all enhance and support this bond.

- **Use short songs and rhymes.** A baby's attention span is generally very short, so quick rhymes and simple songs are often the best for this age.

- **Learn to sing and sign a song or rhyme first.** Once learned, then introduce it to your baby. Some of the songs included may be familiar to you and others may not. To learn to sign the songs or download the music for free, visit www.signtospeak.com. From there, you can download and learn them. If you don't know how to sing a song, just speak the words or chant them.

- **Use exaggerated facial expressions, voices, and signs.** Silliness entertains young children and keeps their attention and interest in an activity.

- **Adapt signs.** Use or adapt signs so they can be performed with one hand. Often you are holding a baby in one arm, so you will have to adapt two-handed signs to work for you.

- **Be tactile.** Touch your child with the signs or with your hands to enhance the playfulness of the activity and to encourage your baby's involvement.

- **Take your baby's hands and help the child make the sign.** Never be forceful. Do this only if your child is involved in the activity. If your baby is distracted or not interested, there will be no benefit.
- **Reward all efforts.** Praise all of your baby's participation.
- **Be creative.** Find other ways to use the signs you learn in the songs throughout the day. For example, you can incorporate them into conversation or in other activities. Adapt songs and rhymes to include signs you are already using.

Creativity

Being creative with singing, rhyming, reading, and other activities keeps them interesting for babies. You can easily do this by adding enthusiasm, facial expressions, and exaggerated signs. You can also take traditional rhymes and familiar songs in new directions. You can change a word here and there to one of more interest for you and your baby. You can even rewrite the words to traditional rhymes and familiar songs.

For example, you can be very creative with "Mary Had a Little Lamb." It can be adapted and used in many different ways. You can creatively use the sign SHEEP by signing it on your baby's arm instead of on your own. See the depiction of SHEEP / LAMB in the Glossary of Signs. You can also change the name from Mary to your baby's name. Or change the lamb to another animal. You can even change all the words while keeping the melody and have a new song. When Ken's grandson, Jacob, was about 14 months old, he liked Ken to sing his own version of "Mary Had a Little Lamb":

> *Jacob had a great big dog, great big dog, great big dog,*
> *Jacob had a great big dog and Zena was her name.*

In this case, Ken signed DOG when he sang it. He later changed it to reflect the pets of his other grandchildren. For example, "Priscilla had a little bunny and Herman was his name." In this case, BUNNY was signed.

You can change and adapt many of the traditional rhymes. Included in the upcoming section are the songs, "Hush Little Baby" and "Sleep Little Baby." The traditional melody of "Hush Little Baby" is the same for both songs, but the words were changed to create a new song in "Sleep Little Baby." Take a look at these two songs for an example of how to change words to fit your circumstances.

A Dozen Songs and Rhymes for Singing

Let's get started singing and signing. The songs and rhymes we have assembled for you are both new and traditional. We have capitalized the words we are suggesting that you sign in each of the rhymes and songs. You can add more words as you become more proficient at singing and signing. It's also fine to reduce the number of signs you use in any of the songs we are providing. Choose what works for you and your baby. More detailed descriptions of each sign used in this section can be found in the Glossary of Signs. To view a demonstration of each of the songs on-line or to download our songs for FREE, go to www.signtospeak.com and use the access code STSB109A. Remember that you can choose to sing, chant or just recite any of the songs. Finally, the sign for SING is the same for SONG. It is a fun sign to learn and use when you are involved in SINGING SONGS with your baby.

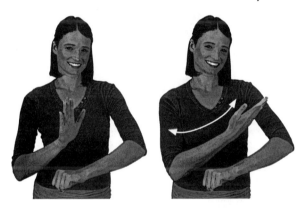

SING/SONG—Extend your left arm with your hand turned downward. Swing your flat right hand back and forth on the left arm in a sweeping motion. Repeat.

Mary Had a Little Lamb

Be Creative: Substitute your baby's name for Mary, and if you've given your baby a name sign, use it here. You can also change the animal to a different one. When you sign LAMB one-handed, move your fingers up your baby's arm, adding touch to the activity.

Mary had a little LAMB,
Little LAMB, little LAMB,
Mary had a little LAMB,
Its FLEECE was white as SNOW.

LAMB

FLEECE

SNOW

Bah, Bah, Black Sheep

Be Creative: In this variation on the original rhyme, we substituted "DADDY," "MOMMY," and "BABY" for "Master," "Dame," and "little boy." You can also substitute name signs you've given to yourselves, your baby, and the baby's siblings. You can even use a variety of animal signs; for example, "one for the ELEPHANT," "one for the MOUSE," "one for the MONKEY who lives down the lane." Additional signs you can add later are ONE and THREE.

Bah, bah, black SHEEP,
Have you any wool? [*sign FLEECE*]
YES Sir, YES Sir,
Three bags full.
One for DADDY,
One for MOMMY,
One for BABY who lives down the lane.
Bah, bah, black SHEEP,
Have you any wool? [*sign FLEECE*]
YES Sir, YES Sir,
Three bags full.

SHEEP

FLEECE

YES

DADDY

MOMMY

BABY

To Market, to Market

(Chanted, spoken, or sung)

Be Creative: Change the animal and sign from pig/hog to something different. For example, change it to cow/calf (sign COW) and use the rhyming words "jiggity jow" and "jiggity jaf" or rabbit/bunny (sign RABBIT) and use the rhyming words "jiggity jabbit" and "jiggity junny."

To market, to market, to buy a fat PIG.
HOME again, HOME again, jiggity jig.

To market, to market, to buy a fat HOG. [*sign PIG*]
HOME again, HOME again, jiggity jog.

PIG/HOG

HOME

Where Is Baby?

(To the melody of "Where Is Thumbkin?")

Be Creative: You can add verses to this song by changing the object in the first two lines; for example, "Where is teddy bear?" or "Where is your dolly?" It is often fun when singing about objects to have them available to hold up. So if you sing "Where is the elephant?" hold up a toy elephant, or "Where is baby's ball?" hold up the ball, and so on. An additional sign you can add later is MOMMY.

WHERE is BABY?
WHERE is BABY?
There YOU are.
There YOU are.
Mommy's GLAD [*sign HAPPY*] to see YOU.
Mommy's GLAD [*sign HAPPY*] to see YOU.
Come and PLAY.
Come and PLAY.

WHERE

BABY

YOU

HAPPY/GLAD

PLAY

How Many Legs?

(Chanted, spoken, or sung)

Be Creative: This rhyme is adaptable to any creatures your baby likes, such as bears, bugs, snakes, snails, and so on. Remember to adapt signs for use with one hand if you are holding your baby. The word NO in this song means to not have any, so we'll use the sign for NONE here. Be tactile with this song. Touch your baby with the sign YOU, and touch or squeeze one leg at a time when you say, "One, two." Additional signs you can add later are ONE, TWO, and FOUR.

COWS they walk on four legs.
MOMMY walks on two.
FISHIES they have no [*sign NONE*] legs.
How many legs have YOU? "One, two."

PUPPIES [*sign DOG*] walk on four legs.
DADDY walks on two.
WHALES they have no [*sign NONE*] legs.
How many legs have YOU? "One, two."

COW

MOMMY

FISH NONE

YOU DADDY

DOG/PUPPY

WHALE

The Tiny Little Mouse

(To the melody of "A Hunting We Will Go")
Be Creative: Make up your own rhymes about other animals, for example,
"The tiny little frog lives upon a log, there he would sing his song," and so on.

The tiny little MOUSE
LOVED his little HOUSE.
There he would EAT and SLEEP
The tiny little MOUSE.

The tiny little CAT
LOVED her little HAT.
She would wear it on her HEAD
The tiny little CAT.

MOUSE

HOUSE

EAT

SLEEP

CAT

LOVE

HAT

HEAD

I See a Bunny

(Chanted, spoken, or sung)

Be Creative: You can substitute any animal for BUNNY and FROG as you sing and sign to this melody. You can also touch your baby with the sign to make the experience more tactile.

I see a BUNNY
LOOKING at YOU.
I see a BUNNY
YES I do.

I see a FROG
LOOKING at YOU.
I see a FROG
YES I do.

BUNNY

LOOK

YOU

YES

FROG

Sleep Little Baby

(To the melody of "Hush Little Baby")

Be Creative: Add the sign for BABY into the song, or change it to your child's name. Change the animals to any that you've learned to sign, such as elephants or horses. You can even change them to objects such as cookies or hats.

SLEEP little *baby* on MOMMY's lap.
SLEEP little *baby* take a NAP.
DREAM of BUNNIES,
DREAM of CATS,
SLEEP little *baby* on MOMMY's lap,
SLEEP little *baby* on MOMMY's lap,

SLEEP/BED/NAP   MOMMY

DREAM

BUNNY   CAT

Five Little Fingers

(Chanted, spoken, or sung)

Be creative: This is a formula song that counts down from five to zero. It can be modified by coming up with new rhymes for the words "four," "three," "two," and "one," and substituting them in the song—"knocking on the floor," "knocking on the sea," "knocking on the shoe," "knocking on a bun," and so on.

FIVE little fingers KNOCKING on the door,
ONE says GOOD-BYE and now there are FOUR.

FOUR little fingers KNOCKING on a tree,
ONE says GOOD-BYE and now there are THREE.

THREE little fingers KNOCKING on you,
ONE says GOOD-BYE and now there are TWO.

TWO little fingers KNOCKING just for fun,
ONE says GOOD-BYE and now there is ONE.

ONE little finger KNOCKING on the run,
ONE says GOOD-BYE and now we're ALL DONE.

FIVE

KNOCKING

ONE

GOOD-BYE

FOUR

THREE

TWO

ALL DONE

The Pretty Little Pony

Be Creative: You can insert any animal that eats grass, such as a lamb or cow. You can also change the lyrics so that you can sing about any animal. For example, you could try, "The pretty little MONKEY, playing on the lawn, eating all the yellow BANANAS, and SLEEPing there 'til dawn."

The pretty little PONY [*sign HORSE*]
PLAYing on the lawn,
EATing all the long green GRASS,
And SLEEPing there 'til dawn.

The pretty little ELEPHANT
PLAYing on the lawn,
EATing all the long green GRASS,
And SLEEPing there 'til dawn.

HORSE/PONY

PLAY

EAT

GRASS

SLEEP

ELEPHANT

Hush Little Baby

Be Creative: Try changing the words you use in the rhyme, as we did in this variation on the original words.

Hush [*sign QUIET*] little BABY, don't say a word.
MOMMY's gonna buy you a mockingBIRD [*sign BIRD*].
And if that mockingBIRD won't SING,
MOMMY's gonna buy you a BELL to ring.
And if that BELL's ring goes away,
MOMMY's gonna say I LOVE YOU every day.
Yes MOMMY's gonna say I LOVE YOU every day.

QUIET/HUSH

BABY

MOMMY

BIRD

SING

BELL

I LOVE YOU

Do You Hear the Ducky Sing?

(Chanted, spoken, or sung to the tune of "Do You Know the Muffin Man?")
Be Creative: Choose any animal you would like to sing about.

Do you HEAR the DUCKY SING?
The DUCKY SING,
The DUCKY SING.
Do you HEAR the DUCKY SING?
Quack, Quack, Quack. [*sign DUCK while making the sound*]

Do you HEAR the MONKEY SING?
The MONKEY SING,
The MONKEY SING.
Do you HEAR the MONKEY SING?
Ook, Ook, Ook. [*sign MONKEY while making the sound*]

HEAR   DUCK

SING   MONKEY

Be Enthusiastic and Supportive

Babies love enthusiasm and happy faces. Keep your singing and signing activities fun and playful. Exaggerate your signs and facial expressions as you sing and sign each song or rhyme. Always give lots of positive reinforcement for your baby's efforts and successes in signing. The sign for GOOD will help you do this.

GOOD—Hold your right hand flat, near your mouth, then move it down to your left hand, which is held with the palm up in front of you. Both palms will be facing up, with the back of your right hand on the palm of your left hand.

Conclusion

By teaching babies several signs from baby-friendly songs and rhymes, parents encourage little ones to become more involved in activities and interested in signs. Babies love to watch and interact with their parents, and before they can sing, hum, or say the words, they will sign. Babies love using their hands for clapping, pointing, waving, and all sorts of finger play associated with rhythm. You can often combine actions and signs in a song to keep it very playful.

Follow your baby's cues. If your baby's attention seems to drift, don't think that your child does not like something; it's simply that babies have short attention spans. Pay attention to this. Be flexible and able to move from one activity to another as you and your baby play and explore our world.

APPENDIX
Babies Can Talk Toolbox

Glossary of Signs

This glossary includes an alphabetical listing of all the signs featured in this book. You can use it for quick reference and to recall any words that you have forgotten. You can also look up words that are of particular interest to you and your baby and then add them to your signing vocabulary.

Here are some tips about signing to help you use the signs in this glossary.

1. Generally, most signs are signed in the area between your shoulders and waist, but for babies it is usually best to keep the signs closer to your face.
2. Use your dominant hand as your main signing hand. If you're left-handed, use your left hand; if you're right-handed, use your right hand.
3. Use facial expressions to clarify meanings. When signing HURT, for example, your facial expression should demonstrate that feeling.
4. Have eye contact. Signing is a visual language and must be seen to be understood.
5. Have fun!

Basic Hand Information

Your hand

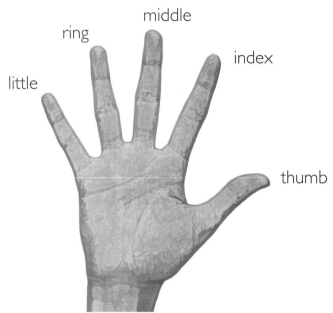

Types of hands

Flat hand

Spread flat with loose fingers

Claw hand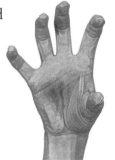

Palm in

Palm out

Palm facing
to the side

Cupped hand

Alphabet

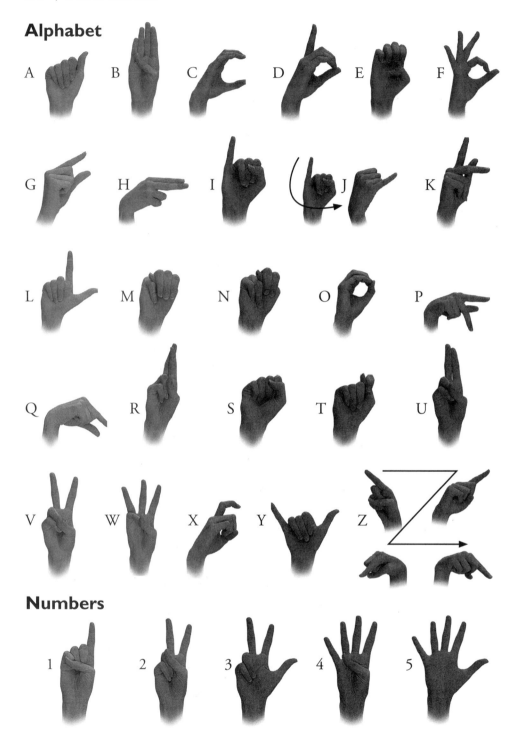

Numbers

All Done / Finished

Hold up both hands with palms in, fingers at chest level, with palms flat and fingers loose. Then, in a quick motion, turn your palms so that they are facing. Repeat.

Angry   *See MAD*

Baby

Fold your arms in front of yourself as if you are holding a baby, and rock them from side to side twice as if you are rocking a baby.

Ball

With your fingers spread and curved, tap the fingertips of both hands together at chest level. Repeat.

Banana

Hold one index finger up, palm forward; then with the other hand, pretend you are peeling a banana from the top of your raised index finger down. The first motion is near the back of the index finger and the second motion is near the front.

Bath

Hold your fists, thumbs up, at the sides of your chest, then rub up and down repeatedly (as if you are washing your chest).

Bed *See SLEEP*

Bell

Hold your left hand up, palm open and facing the right. Make a fist with your right hand, move it back and forth against your left palm.

Bird

Hold your right hand by your mouth, with your index finger and thumb pointed out. Open and close these fingers, imitating the movement of a bird's beak.

Book

Hold your flat hands together at chest level. Open your hands while keeping the little fingers touching (as if you are opening a book).

Bottle

Lay your left hand flat, palm up. Set your right hand on it as if you are holding a bottle, then lift it up, squeezing your hand together, representing how it narrows at the top.

Bunny *See RABBIT*

Cat / Kitty

Make the letter F using both hands, palms facing each other; hold them near the sides of your mouth, and pull outward as if you are tugging on the whiskers of a cat. Repeat.

Caterpillar

Hold one arm out horizontally, and hold the other hand in a fist with your index finger out. Wiggle your index finger as you move your hand up your arm so it looks like a caterpillar crawling along.

Change

Make the letter X with both hands, one on top of the other, with your palms facing each other. Twist your hands so that they switch position. The opposite hand is now on top.

Cold

Make the letter S with both hands and hold them at chest level, palms facing each other. Shake them from side to side with hunched shoulders (as if you are cold).

Cookie

Hold your left hand flat, palm up. Curve the fingers of your right hand so your fingers form a circle (as if holding onto the edges of a round cookie). Then touch your left palm twice, once directly on it and the second twisted slightly so it looks as if you are using a cookie cutter.

Cow

Make the sign for Y with your hand. Hold your thumb on the side of your head and rotate your little finger forward with a twist of your hand (representing the horn on a cow).

Cry

Bring both extended index fingers up to your face, palms facing in, and then move them down your cheeks, alternating sides, as if tears are rolling down your cheeks.

Cup

Hold your left hand flat. Shape your right hand as if you are holding a cup, and then lift it. Repeat.

Daddy *See FATHER*

Diaper

Hold your index and middle fingers out and together with your thumb pointing down, near your waist, and open and close your fingers (as if you are opening and closing a pin on a diaper).

Dog / Puppy

With a flat hand, tap the side of your hip. Then bring your hand up and snap your fingers.

Dream

Make a fist with your index finger pointing out. Hold it next to your temple, palm down, then move outward, bending your finger up and down to indicate that you are thinking.

Drink

Shape your hand as if you are holding a glass, then bring it up to your mouth and tip it toward you so that it looks as if you're drinking from that glass.

Duck

This sign is similar to BIRD. Hold out the index and middle finger of one hand near your mouth, palm facing forward. Open and close them against your thumb. This looks like the wide bill of a duck.

Eat

Hold the thumb and fingertips of one hand together and bring your hand up to your mouth repeatedly (as if you are eating something).

Elephant

Beginning at your nose, move your flat hand, palm out, out and down, indicating the trunk of an elephant.

Elevator

Hold up your flat left hand with the palm facing right. Then make the letter E with your right hand, and move it up and down on your left hand so it looks like an elevator.

Father / Daddy

Tap the thumb of your flat hand, fingers spread and pointing up, on your forehead. Repeat.

Fish

With a flat hand, mimic the movement of a fish as it swims.

Fleece

Hold your hand like a claw, with the palm facing in, near your shoulder. Tap it a few times to represent the wool of a sheep or lamb.

Flower

Hold the fingertips of one hand together (as in the sign for EAT) and touch each side of your nose (as if you are smelling a flower).

Frog

Make the letter S with one hand. Hold it under your chin, and then flick your index and middle fingers out. (This looks like the legs on a frog kicking out.) Repeat.

Gentle

Hold one hand flat, palm down. Then gently stroke the back of that hand.

Girl

Make the sign for the letter A, and hold your hand up to the side of your cheek, then move it down to the chin. Repeat.

Glad *See HAPPY*

Good

Hold your right hand flat, near your mouth, then move it down to your left hand, which is held with the palm up in front of you. Both palms will be facing up, with the back of your right hand on the palm of your left hand.

Good-bye

Hold a flat hand up near your shoulder, palm out. Bend the fingers repeatedly at the knuckle as if you are waving good-bye.

Grass

Hold one hand palm up, with your fingers spread and curved. Starting with the heel of the hand near your chin, move it up and out a bit. Repeat.

Happy

Hold your hands flat, palms in and thumbs up. Brush your chest in a circular motion. Use with a happy facial expression. Repeat.

Hat

Pat the top of your head twice with a flat hand.

Head

With a bent hand, fingers together, touch the side of your forehead and then move down to touch the side of your chin.

Hear

Extend an index finger, and touch it to your ear.

Help

Hold one hand in a fist, thumb up, and the other hand flat, palm up. Lay your fist on top of your palm. Then lift both hands (as if one hand is helping the other). Use only your fist hand whenever you cannot make a two-handed sign.

Hog *See PIG*

Home

Holding fingertips together (as in EAT), palm down, touch the side of your chin near your mouth and then up to the top of your cheek. (Home is where you eat and sleep.)

Horse / Pony

Make a fist with your thumb out and your index and middle fingers up. Hold the thumb at the side of your head, and bend your index and middle fingers up and down twice (like the ears of a horse).

Hot

Hold your curved hand, fingers spread, near your mouth, palm in. Then, in a quick motion, pull your hand away, turning it outward and down a little (as if you're getting rid of something hot very fast).

House

With the fingertips of your hands touching, move your flat hands from the center of the "roof" out to the "walls" and then down (as if you are drawing the outline of the roof and walls of a house).

Hurt / Ouch

With both hands in fists, point index fingers toward each other and tap the fingertips together. Remember that this sign is directional. Sign it near the place where you hurt.

Hush   *See QUIET*

I / Me

Hold a fist up with your index finger out, and point it to the middle of your chest.

I Love You

(shorthand, slang version)

Hold your hand up near your shoulder, palm out, with your ring and middle fingers down, your index and little fingers up, and your thumb out. Keep this sign stationary; if you move it around, you could be signing JET. Sometimes movement changes the meaning of a sign.

Jump

Hold one hand flat with your palm up. Extend the index and middle fingers of the other hand out to represent legs, and place them on the flat hand. Then make the motion of jumping up from your flat hand.

Kitty   *See CAT*

Knock

Hold your left flat hand up, facing to the right, then knock on it with your right fist as if you are knocking on a door.

Lamb *See SHEEP*

Listen

Hold a cupped hand up near your ear (as if you are trying to listen).

Look

Make the letter V, palm down, your fingertips touching your cheek just under the eye. Then move your hand out in the direction of what you are looking at (as if your fingertips are an extension of your eyes).

Love

Make fists, crossed at the wrist, and hold them against your chest (as if you are holding something you love).

Mad / Angry

Hold your hand up with the fingertips curved, palm in front of your chin. Then squeeze your fingers together just a little and move your hand slightly toward your chin. Use an angry facial expression.

Me *See I / Me*

Milk

Squeeze your hand repeatedly (as if you are milking a cow).

Mommy   *See MOTHER*

Monkey

With both hands curved, palms in, scratch your sides twice in an upward movement (like a monkey scratching itself).

Moon

Hold a fist with your thumb and index finger out and curved (as if you are making the letter C), then tap the side of your head with your thumb. This looks like a crescent moon. Repeat.

More

Hold the fingertips of both hands together (as you do with one hand for EAT) and then tap them together. Repeat.

Mother / Mommy

Tap the thumb of your flat hand, fingers spread, on your chin. Repeat.

Mouse

Brush your index finger twice across the tip of your nose.

Nap *See SLEEP*

None

Make the letter O with both hands, palms out, at chest level. Wave your hands from side to side repeatedly.

Pig / Hog

Hold the back of a flat hand under your chin. Bend your fingers at the knuckles, and move them up and down twice.

Play

Make the letter Y with both hands, palms up, then twist them at the wrist to turn the palms up and down repeatedly.

Pony *See HORSE*

Puppy *See DOG*

Quiet / Hush

Hold flat hands, up near your mouth, palms facing sideways, crossed at the wrists. Then, in a quick sweeping motion, move your hands down and apart, stopping at the waist with palms facing down.

Rabbit / Bunny

Cross both hands at the wrist with your index and middle fingers and thumb extended. Bend your fingers up and down with a double motion (like the ears on a bunny).

Read

Hold your left hand up, your palm facing to the right. With the other hand, make the letter V, point the fingertips toward your left hand, and then move them from side to side and down (as if the right hand is reading words in a book).

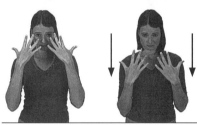

Sad

Hold your hands flat, fingers spread and palms facing in, at eye level and then move them down a little. Use with a sad facial expression.

Say

With your index finger out, touch it to your chin just below your lips, pointing to your mouth. Repeat.

Sheep / Lamb

Hold your left hand flat with your arm across your body. Make the letter V with your right hand, palm up, and open and close your extended fingers as you move them up your arm from the hand to the elbow (as if you are cutting the wool off a sheep).

Sign

Make fists with both hands, extend the index fingers, and hold them pointing up. Then move your hands in large, alternating circles toward your chest.

Sing / Song

Extend your left arm with your hand turned downward. Swing your flat right hand back and forth on the left arm in a sweeping motion. Repeat.

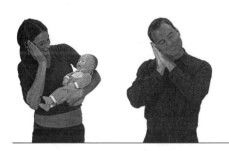

Sleep / Bed / Nap

With your head bent, close your eyes and rest your cheek on the palm of your flat hand (as if you are pretending to be asleep). You may also encounter this as a two-handed sign, with both hands held together and under a cheek. Either version is fine.

Smile

Hold flat hands slightly bent, with your fingertips near the sides of your mouth. Then move your hands up each side of your cheeks (as if you are drawing a smile).

Snow

Hold your hands flat, palms down and fingers spread, at head level. Then lower them slowly as you wiggle your fingers (like snow falling to the ground).

Song *See SING*

Spoon

Hold your left hand flat, palm up and slightly cupped. With your right hand make the letter U and make a scooping motion down, across, and up from the left hand. It will look as if you are using a spoon. Repeat.

Tired

Hold your hands flat, bent at the knuckles, with the palms facing in, fingertips touching at your shoulders. Roll your hands downward on your fingertips. Use with a tired facial expression and posture.

Train

Make the sign for the letter U with both hands, holding your palms down. Lay the fingers of your right hand on top of the fingers of your left. Then move the right-hand fingers back and forth on the left-hand fingers. Repeat.

Tree

Hold your left arm across your body, palm down. Place the elbow of your right arm on top of your left hand, with your right hand flat, pointing up with loose fingers and facing left. Twist your right hand back and forth. This sign looks like a tree. Repeat.

Wash

Make fists with both hands, right palm down and left palm up. Rub the right hand in a circular motion over the left hand. Repeat.

Whale

Hold your left arm with a flat hand across your body to represent the surface of the ocean. Make the sign for the letter Y with your right hand and move it down and up (going above and below the "water line") from your elbow to your hand so it looks like a whale's tail moving up and down in the water.

Where

Hold your index finger up and wave it from side to side.

Yes

Make the letter S with one hand, palm down. Then move it up and down at the wrist (like a head nodding yes).

You

Make a fist hand, and point your index finger out and toward the person to whom you are talking.

Resources

As you continue to sign with your baby, you'll find these books and Web sites helpful.

Books

Apel, Kenn, and Julie J. Masterson. *Beyond Baby Talk: From Sounds to Sentences—A Parent's Complete Guide to Learning Language Development.* Roseville, CA: Prima Publishing, 2001.

Costello, Elaine. *Random House Webster's American Sign Language Dictionary.* New York: Random House, 1998.

Daniels, Marilyn. *Benedictine Roots in the Development of Deaf Education: Listening with the Heart.* Westport, CT: Bergin and Garvey, 1997.

Daniels, Marilyn. *Dancing with Words: Signing for Hearing Children's Literacy.* Westport, CT: Bergin and Garvey, 2001.

Fisch, Shalom M. *Children's Learning from Educational Television—Sesame Street and Beyond.* Mahwah, NJ: Erlbaum Associates, 2004.

Greenspan, Stanley I. *The Growth of the Mind and the Endangered Origins of Intelligence.* Cambridge, MA: Perseus Books, 1997.

Habermeyer, Sharlene. *Good Music Brighter Children.* Rocklin, CA: Prima Publishing, 1999.

Holt, John. *How Children Learn.* Cambridge, MA: Perseus Books, 1983.

Hughes, Fergus P. *Children, Play, and Development.* 3rd Ed. Boston, MA: Allyn and Bacon, 1999.

Leach, Penelope. *Your Baby and Child—From Birth to Age Five.* New York: Alfred A. Knopf, 1990.

On the Web

www.wesign.com
www.signtospeak.com
ASL Browser at http://commtechlab.msu.edu/sites/aslweb/browser.htm
www.Aslpro.com
www.Handspeak.com
www.dictionaryofsign.com

Free Downloads and More

www.signtospeak.com
www.wesign.com

Toolbox Handouts

Included in this Toolbox are pages that you can use for quick reference. We have provided you with 12 tips for successful signing with a baby along with 12 tips for signing and singing songs. We also compiled a list of 12 useful signs as a quick reference page for you to photocopy, for personal use only, and place around the house or to offer to other family members and caregivers in order to help them become involved in the signing process.

12 Tips for Successful Signing with Babies

1. Have your baby's attention.

2. Place signs near your face.

3. Enunciate words clearly, and sign correct ASL signs.

4. Incorporate signing into your everyday life.

5. Consistently sign the word every time you say it.

6. Use strong and exaggerated voice and facial expressions.

7. Relate your signs to the words or objects you are using.

8. Keep signing a simple, fun, and playful activity.

9. Be creative and create lots of signing opportunities.

10. Get everyone involved in signing.

11. Give lots of positive reinforcement.

12. Be patient. Generally babies will sign back to you between 9 and 14 months old.

12 Tips for Signing
with Songs and Rhymes

1. Have your baby's attention.

2. Follow your baby's cues. Be ready to change to any other song or activity that draws your baby's interest.

3. Keep the activity simple.

4. Keep the activity fun and playful. Be full of enthusiasm.

5. Keep songs short. Rhymes are often the best.

6. Learn to sing and sign a song or rhyme before introducing it to your baby. Chant or recite songs if it's easier.

7. Use exaggerated facial expressions, voices, and signs.

8. If necessary, adapt signs so they can be performed with one hand.

9. Be tactile, and touch your baby with the signs.

10. Help your baby to form the signs, but don't be forceful.

11. Praise all of your baby's efforts.

12. Be creative. Change the signs and words in the songs and rhymes to fit your baby's interests, and try to use the signs at other times during the day.

12 Everyday Signs

Photocopy and hang up for your quick signing reference.

Eat

More

All Done

Hurt / Ouch

Sleep / Bed / Nap

I Love You

Mommy

Daddy

Bath

Gentle

Change / Diaper

Good

Notes

Chapter 3

1. Michael C. Corballis, "The Gestural Origins of Language," *American Scientist* 87, no. 2 (1999): 138–45.
2. Corballis, "The Gestural Origins of Language," 141.
3. Katherine Nelson, "The Role of Language in Infant Development," in *Psychological Development from Infancy: Image to Intention,* ed. M. Bornstein and W. Kenne (Hillsdale, NJ: Erlbaum Associates, 1979).
4. Lauren B. Adamson, Robert Bakeman, and C. B. Smith, "Gestures, Words, and Early Object Sharing," in *From Gesture to Language in Hearing and Deaf Children,* ed. Virginia Volterra and Carol J. Erting (Washington, DC: Gallaudet University Press, 1994).
5. Alan Fogel, "The Ontogeny of Gestural Communication: The First Six Months," in *Language Behavior in Infancy and Early Childhood*, ed. R. E. Stark (New York: Elsevier, 1981).
6. Colwyn Trevarthen, "Communication and Cooperation in Early Infancy: A Description of Primary Inter-subjectivity," in *Before Speech,* ed. M. Bullowa (New York: Cambridge University Press, 1979).
7. Jean Piaget, *The Origins of Intelligence in Children* (New York: Norton, 1952).
8. Jean Piaget, *The Language and Thought of the Child* (Cleveland, OH: World Publishing, 1955).
9. Barbara Schaeffer, "Teaching Spontaneous Sign Language to Nonverbal Children: Theory and Method," *Sign Language Studies,* no. 21 (1978): 317–52.
10. Daniel E. Lieberman, Robert C. McCarthy, and Karen M. Hiiemae, "Ontogeny of Postnatal Hyoid and Larynx Descent in Humans," *Oral Biology* 46 no. 2 (2001): 117–28.
11. Frank R. Wilson, *The Hand: How Its Use Shapes the Brain, Language, and Human Culture* (New York: Pantheon Books, 1998).
12. Wilson, *The Hand,* 188.
13. Marilyn Daniels, *Dancing with Words: Signing for Hearing Children's Literacy* (Westport, CT: Bergin and Garvey, 2001): 130.

Chapter 4

1. William C. Stokoe, "The Once New Field: Sign Language Research or Breaking Sod in the Back Forty," *Sign Language Studies,* no. 93 (1996): 388.
2. William C. Stokoe, *Language in Hand: Why Sign Came Before Speech* (Washington, DC: Gallaudet University Press, 2001): 176–77.
3. Stokoe, *Language in Hand,* 178.

Chapter 8

1. Howard Gardner, *Intelligence Reframed* (New York: Basic Books, 1999): 150.

Chapter 9

1. Fergus P. Hughes, *Children, Play, and Development,* 3rd ed. (Boston: Allyn and Bacon, 1995): 189.

Bibliography

Adamson, Lauren B., Robert Bakeman, and C. B. Smith. "Gestures, Words, and Early Object Sharing." In *From Gesture to Language in Hearing and Deaf Children,* edited by Virginia Volterra and Carol J. Erting. Washington, DC: Gallaudet University Press, 1994.

Brisbane, Holly E. *The Developing Child.* Woodland Hills, CA: Glencoe/McGraw-Hill, 2006.

Corballis, Michael C. "The Gestural Origins of Language." *American Scientist* 87, no. 2 (1999).

Daniels, Marilyn. *Dancing with Words: Signing for Hearing Children's Literacy.* Westport, CT: Bergin and Garvey, 2001.

Fogel, Alan. "The Ontogeny of Gestural Communication: The First Six Months." In *Language Behavior in Infancy and Early Childhood,* edited by R. E. Stark. New York: Elsevier, 1981.

Gardner, Howard. *Intelligence Reframed.* New York: Basic Books, 1999.

Holt, John. *How Children Learn.* Rev. ed. Cambridge, MA: Perseus Books, 1983.

Hughes, Fergus P. *Children, Play, and Development.* 3rd ed. Boston, MA: Allyn and Bacon, 1995.

Lieberman, Daniel E., Robert C. McCarthy, and Karen M. Hiiemae. "Ontogeny of Postnatal Hyoid and Larynx Descent in Humans." *Oral Biology* 46, no. 2 (2001).

Nelson, Katherine. "The Role of Language in Infant Development." In *Psychological Development from Infancy: Image to Intention,* edited by M. Bornstein and W. Kenne. Hillsdale, NJ: Erlbaum Associates, 1979.

Piaget, Jean. *The Language and Thought of the Child.* Cleveland, OH: World Publishing, 1955.

Piaget, Jean. *The Origins of Intelligence in Children.* New York: Norton, 1952.

Schaeffer, Barbara. "Teaching Spontaneous Sign Language to Nonverbal Children: Theory and Method." *Sign Language Studies,* no. 21 (1978).

Stokoe, William C. *Language in Hand: Why Sign Came Before Speech.* Washington, DC: Gallaudet University Press, 2001.

Stokoe, William C. *Sign Language Structures.* Silver Springs. MD: Linstock Press, 1960.

Stokoe, William C. "The Once New Field: Sign Language Research or Breaking Sod in the Back Forty." *Sign Language Studies,* no. 93 (1996).

Trevarthen, Colwyn. "Communication and Cooperation in Early Infancy: A Description of Primary Inter-subjectivity." In *Before Speech,* edited by M. Bullowa. New York: Cambridge University Press, 1979.

Wilson, Frank R. *The Hand: How Its Use Shapes the Brain, Language, and Human Culture.* New York: Pantheon Books, 1998.

Published Studies of Dr. Marilyn Daniels

The following are all studies that demonstrate increased vocabulary growth for hearing children through the use of sign.

Daniels, M. "ASL as a Factor in Acquiring English." *Sign Language Studies* 22, no. 78 (1993): 23–29.

Daniels, M. "The Effect of Sign Language on Hearing Children's Language Development." *Communication Education,* 43, no. 4 (1994): 291–298.

Daniels, M. "Words More Powerful Than Sound." *Sign Language Studies* 23, no. 83 (1994): 155–156.

Daniels, M. "Bilingual, Bimodal Education for Hearing Kindergarten Students." *Sign Language Studies* 25, no. 90 (1996): 25–37.

Daniels, M. "Seeing Language: The Effect Over Time of Sign Language on Vocabulary Development in Early Childhood Education." *Child Study Journal* 26, no. 3 (1996): 193–208.

Daniels, M. "Teacher Enrichment of Prekindergarten Curriculum with Sign Language." *Journal of Research in Childhood Education* 12, no. 1 (1997): 27–33.

Daniels, M. "Sign Language Advantage." *Sign Language Studies* 2, no. 1 (2001): 5–19.

Daniels, M. "Sign Education: A Communication Tool for Young Learners." *Speech Communication Association of Pennsylvania Annual* 57 (2001): 77–95.

Daniels, M., "Reading Signs: A Way to Promote Early Childhood Literacy." *Communication Teacher* 16, no. 2 (2002): 32–38.

Daniels, M. "Using a Signed Language as a Second Language for Kindergarten Students." *Child Study Journal* 3, no. 1 (2003): 53–70.

Daniels, M. "American Sign Language as a Second Language for Hearing Kindergarten Students." *Communication Education.* In press.

Daniels, M. "The Silent Signs of Learning: ASL in a Special Needs Class." *Child Study Journal.* In press.

Daniels, M. "Relationship between the Use of American Sign Language and Students' Self-esteem and Spelling Performance in a Learning Support Class." *Qualitative Research Reports in Communication.* In press.

Index

About the Authors

Dr. Marilyn Daniels

Dr. Marilyn Daniels

Since the 1990s, Dr. Marilyn Daniels has been one of the premier authors and researchers on the use of American Sign Language with hearing children. She has been quoted extensively in many publications and has appeared on radio and television for over 20 years. She is a professor of communication arts and sciences at Pennsylvania State University.

Her first study, "ASL as a Factor in Acquiring English," was published in *Sign Language Studies* in 1993. Since then she has published 19 additional research studies and two books on this subject, including her widely quoted book *Dancing with Words: Signing for Hearing Children's Literacy.* She has been in numerous magazines and newspapers in the United States, Canada, and England. Marilyn also lectures and presents workshops to help parents, teachers, and other caregivers learn how to effectively use sign language with hearing children.

Her research has taken place in a variety of locations in the United States, from Vermont to California. In addition, she has been actively involved in several sign language projects throughout the world. Recently, she introduced the Canadian Association for the Deaf and Hard of Hearing to the ASL literacy process that she is engaged in with hearing children in the United States.

She has served as a consultant to several ongoing sign language projects in the United Kingdom. In these endeavors, British Sign Language is being used to improve learning with young students. In addition, she taught summer courses at Nagoya University in Nagoya, Japan, to teachers of English as a second language.

Ken Frawley

Ken Frawley graduated from California State University, Fullerton with a bachelor's degree in liberal studies, intending to become an elementary school teacher. Instead, he began to perform, often with his wife, Georgia, at children's and family concerts at schools, libraries, and community events throughout Southern California. He has written over 200 children's songs used around the country and is an award-winning producer of video products for children. He has taught thousands of parents and teachers across the country how to incorporate singing and signing into the lives of children, from birth to elementary school. He has performed his play-along and signing songs with hundreds of thousands of children for many years. In addition, he coproduced the multiple award-winning *Say, Sing and Sign* video and the We Sign DVD series.

Ken and Georgia Frawley

He and Georgia experienced the benefits of signing with their own children in the 1980s. They used sign not only to enhance communication, but as part of songs and games that provided for fun family interaction while supporting early learning of educational concepts. They later included signing activities in their children's concerts and shows. From these experiences they developed programs for using sign with all hearing children, from babies to elementary school ages, and have taught their concepts and techniques to parents and educators across the country.

Georgia Frawley

Georgia Frawley, MA, began working as a dorm counselor at the California School for the Deaf in Riverside, California, while she was finishing her teaching credential in physical education and home economics from California State Polytechnic University, Pomona. By the end of her first day of work, the children had taught her over 30 signs.

When she married Ken and they had a daughter, Coreen, signing with her was second nature to Georgia. As she talked, Georgia also signed the same words she had learned to use with the children from the School for the Deaf. It seemed to her that she was supporting language growth by making words visual for her young child.

She has been teaching Child Development, Parenting, and Marriage and Family classes for over 30 years. While developing and running her on-campus day-care center, she received a masters degree in counseling, which she used to help the young parents at her high school. She has taught thousands of students and parents about the benefits of sign language and how to use signing effectively with young children.

About Production Associates

Production Associates has become a leader in producing quality educational video and DVD products for children from birth through elementary school. Since the early 1990s it has developed audio and video titles that have been sold across the United States. Its projects have included pilots for television, including a Russian language children's show, children's exercise videos, and phonemic awareness products. Hundreds of the songs it has produced for children are available on iTunes.

For over 15 years, the products developed by Production Associates have been highly acclaimed by parents, teachers, caregivers, and other early childhood professionals. The company has received over 50 national awards for its children's and family products.

Production Associates' first collection of sign language products was called Say, Sing and Sign, later to become the We Sign series. Since the beginning, each product and every song has been selected to support communication, learning, and language development; enhance vocabulary; and, above all, provide adults and children with fun, playful, and bonding activities.

The We Sign series has always featured American Sign Language. ASL is one of the most common languages in the country, and because of its movement and visual nature, it provides a wonderful way for children to be involved in their learning. We Sign uses an official language rather than made-up signs or gestures because ASL offers the structure and vocabulary of a language and hearing children receive many benefits through the use of signing.

Production Associates has sought not only to create a greater awareness regarding the use of signing with hearing children but also to develop signing activities that engage children. One of its goals has been to produce television products that create doers, not just viewers. The We Sign series encourages children to follow along, sing along, and sign along. Another goal is to promote signing to parents, teachers, and caregivers as a way to create playful learning and bonding interaction.

Now with the addition of the Sign to Speak books to the We Sign family, Production Associates is seeking to help parents, teachers, and other adults to become more proficient with signing, as well as to become educated about the science behind signing success. All these efforts are geared toward allowing children to get a "Jump Start on Smart," getting them started in school with a language-rich foundation that will help them succeed, increasing their learning confidence, and developing an interest in learning that will last a lifetime.

We Sign Family of Products

The We Sign Early Learning and Communication collection of DVDs features American Sign Language, instruction, and songs. These products are ideal for parents, teachers, and caregivers to use with children of all ages for interactive sing and sign along activities.

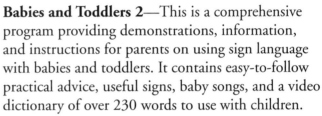

Babies and Toddlers 2—This is a comprehensive program providing demonstrations, information, and instructions for parents on using sign language with babies and toddlers. It contains easy-to-follow practical advice, useful signs, baby songs, and a video dictionary of over 230 words to use with children.

Baby Songs—Ideal signing songs for parents to use with babies. Features all the songs found in *Babies Can Talk.*

Play Time—Fun interactive songs, featuring the We Sign Kids, for young children and their parents, families, and caregivers to sing and sign together. Songs included are "The Wheels on the Bus," "One Little Kitty," "This is the Way We Wash Our Hands," "If You're Happy and You Know It," "A Really Good Treat," "Stop, Look, and Listen," "Jacob Wore a Red Hat," "Jumping," and "Raindrops."

Fun Time—Energetic songs, featuring the We Sign Kids, that involve children and families in singing and signing activities. Songs included are "Five Little Monkeys," "I See, I Hear, I Smell," "Old MacDonald," "Little Miss Muffet," "I'm Gonna Play," "A Little Song in My Heart," "If I Were a Little Fish," "Mama I'm Readin'," "The More We Get Together," "Oh Where, Oh Where," and "Row, Row, Row Your Boat."

Special features include Spanish language tracks, closed captioning, subtitles, and a song jukebox.

Special features include We Sign Kids track, instructor track, Spanish language track, subtitles, closed captioning, and a song jukebox.

WeSign.com

A B C—Songs included are the "ABC Song," "ABC Object Song," and "S M I L E." Ideal for letter and sound recognition and spelling fun.

Numbers—Songs included are "One, Two, Buckle My Shoe," "The Number Song," "Ten to One Hundred," "Numbers and Things," "One Little Bird," and "One Fuzzy Caterpillar." An ideal way to learn numbers from 1 to 100 along with lots of vocabulary.

Colors—Songs included are "The Color Song," "Mixing All My Colors," "Let My Colors Flow," "The Snowman's Hat," and "Colors and Things." Learning about colors with signed songs is fun.

Rhymes—Songs included are "Mary Had a Little Lamb," "Twinkle, Twinkle Little Star," "Old Mother Hubbard," "It's Raining, It's Pouring," "Humpty Dumpty," "Rock-A-Bye Baby," "Little Bo Peep," "Wee Willie Winkie," "Little Jack Horner," and "Three Blind Mice." Children learn these classic rhymes as they sing and sign along.

Animals—Songs included are "Oh Where, Oh Where Has My Little Dog Gone," "Itsy Bitsy Spider," "Bat, Bat," "The Bear Went Over the Mountain," "Croak, Said the Toad," "Animal Parade," "Froggie Went A-Courtin'," and "Animal Alphabet." Playful animal songs for vocabulary building.

WeSign.com

Classroom Favorites—Songs included are "Bingo," "Twinkle, Twinkle Little Star," "I Saw a Ship A-Sailing," "Earth, Earth, Earth," "Home on the Range," "This is the Way We Wash Our Hands," "Jingle Bells," "One Little," and "There Was an Old Woman." Comes with We Sign Kids track, Spanish language track, subtitles, and closed captioning.

More Animals—Songs included are "Animals Live All Around the World," "Thinking of an Animal," "They Call Home," and "Walking Through the Forest." Elementary children learn signs for animals along with lots of vocabulary. Comes with We Sign Kids track, Spanish language track, subtitles, and closed captioning.

Santa's Favorite Christmas Songs—Songs included are "Jingle Bells," "O Christmas Tree," "Up on the House Top," "Jolly Old St. Nicholas," "There Is Snow on the Mountain," "The Twelve Days of Christmas," and "We Wish You a Merry Christmas." Great songs for all ages.

Christmas Carols—Christmas carols included are "Silent Night," "Away in a Manger," "O Little Town of Bethlehem," "What Child Is This?" "Joy to the World," "God Rest Ye Merry, Gentlemen," and "O Come, All Ye Faithful." All ages love to sing and sign along to these classic carols.

American Patriotic Songs—Songs included are "Yankee Doodle," "America," "Grand Old Flag," "America the Beautiful," "Battle Hymn of the Republic," "Yankee Doodle Boy," "God Bless America," and "The Star Spangled Banner." Also featured on this DVD is the Pledge of Allegiance.

Sign to Speak On-Line

Free on-line support is available with your book. Simply go to http://www.signtospeak.com and log in with the code STSB109A to access a variety of additional resources.

FREE On-Line Music Downloads

Use your log-in code to listen to and download all the songs found in this book. Play them at home, in the car, or anywhere else you would like. Sing the melodies with your baby as often as you can.

FREE On-Line Video Demonstrations

• Signing music videos of all the songs in this book
• A signing video dictionary of all the signs featured
  Simply use your log-in code to watch and learn from our video presentations. Discover how to sing and sign each of the songs and watch how any sign you are interested in is formed.

FREE On-Line Sheet Music Downloads

If you would like the sheet music so you can learn to sing and play the songs found in this book, just use your log-in code and download the music.

FREE On-Line Journal Page Samples

If you would like some ideas for your journal pages, we have provided several samples for you to use on our Web site. (You can download the pages with your log-in code.)